Drama

ANDREW BROWN

Drama

with an introduction by
SIR TYRONE GUTHRIE

ARC BOOKS, Inc.
New York

PUBLISHED BY ARC BOOKS, Inc.

480 Lexington Avenue, New York 17, N. Y.

© ANDREW BROWN 1962

Library of Congress Catalog Card No.: 62-17581

Printed in The United States of America

Contents

Acknowledgements

THE author wishes to make acknowledgements to the authors and publishers concerned for permission to include extracts from the following works:

George Bernard Shaw, by G. K. Chesterton, John Lane, The Bodley Head; *Prince of Players, Edwin Booth*, by Eleanor Ruggles, Peter Davies; *A Year's Course in Speech Training* by Anne McAllister, University of London Press; 'When You Are Old' from *The Complete Poems of W. B. Yeats*, reprinted by permission of Mrs W. B. Yeats, and Macmillan & Co.; 'The Tunnel' by Mabel Constanduros and Howard Agg, from *Dialogue and Drama*, Wm. Heinemann; *The Definitive Edition of Rudyard Kipling's Verse*, Mrs Brampton and Hodder & Stoughton; *No Time for Comedy*, copyright 1938, 1939 by S. N. Behrmann, reprinted by permission of Brandt & Brandt and Hamish Hamilton; an article by Herbert Luthy from *Encounter* (July 1956); and an article by Henry Adler from *The Twentieth Century* (August 1956).

Introduction

THERE is no right way of acting or directing a play, any more than there is a single right way of hammering a nail or boiling an egg. But some of the many possible ways are righter than others and some are more wrong.

Andrew Brown has sensibly avoided any dogmatic statements about right and wrong. Out of a long experience of both the professional and the amateur theatre, he offers advice, which is not too abstruse for beginners, nor too elementary for those who have some experience but are not on that account too proud, or too dull, to learn.

I especially like what he has to say about the use of the voice. Clear and expressive speech is the greatest asset which an actor can possess. It is far more important to speak well than to look well. Unless you actually are physically deformed, you can make yourself up to look handsome and attractive, old or young, gentle or fierce. But there is no great advantage in looking right unless you can, first, make people hear what you say; and, second, make it sound sufficiently interesting for them to want to listen.

You cannot, in my opinion, teach people to act, unless they have a certain aptitude, unless they have the sort of imagination which enables them to pretend to be somebody, or something, which in fact they are not. But you can teach a person a very great deal about clear and expressive speech—a most important advantage, by the way, not just to actors but to people in every and in any walk of life.

You will find Andrew Brown a most helpful mentor in this department. He tells you what to do, and what not to do, in clear, simple language, no high-flown, pretentious jargon. He also suggests practical exercises, which will, I guarantee, once you have mastered them, leave you a clearer and more expressive speaker.

TYRONE GUTHRIE

CHAPTER ONE

Acting—the young beginner

ALLOWING for the inevitable exception, it is assumed that beginners, in acting as in most things, are comparatively young. People can start acting from scratch at almost any age, but generally speaking, youth has the advantage both of greater mental flexibility and physical agility. Habits and mannerisms have not become ingrained. Adaptability is easier. Switching from one idea to another requires less effort. Acquiring new techniques is more of an adventure than an irksome necessity. The younger a person is the less he has to unlearn.

The younger an actor starts, the better his chances are of eventually becoming a good as well as an experienced actor, though the two do not necessarily go together. So the first thing you must do is to get on to the stage in front of an audience as soon as you can, without demanding too high a standard from your early theatrical environment. You cannot afford to be too critical until you have had at least a little experience. Never miss an opportunity of seeing a professional production. Try to watch the best actors from the auditorium, but be prepared to go on the stage with the worst, if that is the only way you can start to get practice. You may console yourself with the knowledge that the best actors are not always the best companions.

Listen to what everybody interested in the theatre has to say and find out how it applies to you. Don't try to remember it all. Make notes of what you consider important or relevant to the purpose of acting. When you get a foothold, never argue with your producer if you disagree with him, not even if he is palpably wrong.

A good producer will invite discussion, but few will welcome interruptions of actual rehearsals.

There can be no generalizations or hard and fast rules about acting or production and any suggestions made after this statement are no more than pointers for the guidance of beginners culled from a considerable experience learned the hard way. There is, however, much good advice to be had for the asking from people who have been successful. Even that of some who have failed is not always to be discounted. Those who have

9

produced even mediocre results are worthier of attention than those with only brilliant theories to expound. The man who offers you 'technique' might be a safer bet than the one who brings you 'The Method'. Technique means simply the general principles of the craft. When you have mastered these you will work out your own method.

Let us consider the technique of the actor, broadly at first and in some detail later.

To begin with, we shall allow ourselves the privilege of over-simplification and say that acting is a combination of imagination, speech and movement. We give expression to ideas through the medium of the spoken word, to which gesture and facial expression are auxiliaries. But if acting required nothing more than the ability to speak and move about on a stage, anyone and every-body, except the dumb and the paralysed, would be able to act. Even the varying degrees in the power of expression among normal people do not explain the difference between those who can act and those who can't. So we must examine the application of speech and movement to two different sets of circumstances; those of everyday communications and of theatrical interpreta-tion.

In ordinary conversation we choose our words to communicate our own ideas. Some people think more clearly than others and consequently find a readier means of expression. Others are better educated and have a better choice of words, although fluency is often as much a matter of temperament as of education. Actors are not noticeably better general conversationalists than, say, teachers or businessmen. Yet words are the tools of their trade to a greater extent. But whose words? The good teacher will choose his own words for the interpretation of his subject to his class. No matter how brilliant or famous the actor, he is limited to the words of his author when playing to an audience. His very manner of expressing the author's words is often, if not dictated, at least tempered by the will of the producer. The teacher is at liberty to choose between several combinations or groups of words for expressing a single idea. The most an actor can do is to find different ways of expressing the same words in the same order for the best way of interpreting the meaning.

There is a considerable difference between these two approaches to speech. If we listen to an extempore radio or television talk, between an actor and an academic, we are not surprised if the latter provides the more lucid or convincing argument and we should expect a well-modulated voice and better enunciation from the actor, even without rehearsal. On the other hand, we might be tempted to switch off if the academic were to attempt a sight-reading of a speech from *Hamlet*, no matter how eloquently he could discuss the play in his own words.

The actor must learn to listen as well as to speak. He has to study delicate nuances of emphasis and subtle shades of intonation. In speech the simple word 'Yes' can mean anything from simple affirmation to complete denial. In fact, it can mean 'No'. If you were a poor young bank clerk and you asked the chairman of your bank for permission to marry his daughter, he could say 'Yes' in such a way that it would not be necessary for him to add 'Over my dead body' for you to guess his meaning. The word would come instinctively from him, the spontaneous expression of a mixture of emotions: rage, revulsion, surprise, fear . . . but if you tried to imitate exactly his manner of saying it, in retrospect on the stage, you would have difficulty in doing so. You are not the father of that girl. You didn't feel the shock of *his* little world crumbling under *your* feet. But if you are to act, you will have to try to penetrate the dim recesses of that man's mind, to understand his prejudices, his snobbery, a father's feeling of protection for his daughter. You will have to feel the quickening of the heart beat, the spasm of the diaphragm, the raised blood-pressure. In short, you will have to find out what made him say 'Yes'—just like that—when what he meant was 'No'.

Purposeful listening is a habit which can be learned by concentration, and it has offshoots which are worth the effort and are vital to the actor: insight, sensitivity, sympathy, an extra awareness and a quickening of the spirit. When we listen to anything better than small talk, to a reasoned, closely-knit exposition, we find it difficult to concentrate for longer than a few minutes at a time, so that we are left with gaps in our memory of the argument. We are often unable to assess the exact meaning of even a simple sentence and if we were to repeat it we might give a totally wrong impression of the original speaker's intention. We have misheard a particular inflection of the voice or emphasis on a word. If, then, we are capable of misinterpreting the living spoken word, how much more difficult it must be to interpret correctly the dead letter of the printed text. When a script is read, even silently, it must be 'heard' with the inner ear, as well as seen. Those black symbols on the white background are almost meaningless until they have life breathed into them by the human voice.

Before we go into the intricacies of dialogue in true drama take the simplest possible example. Look at this sentence:

'Tom Jones caught that rabbit.'

What does it mean? What it says? But *it says* very little! Which of the following does it mean? The implication, unstated, is in brackets.

Tom Jones caught that rabbit	(Not his brother, Jim)
Tom *Jones* caught that rabbit	(Not Tom Smith)
Tom Jones *caught* that rabbit	(He didn't steal it)
Tom Jones caught *that* rabbit	(Not the one over there)
Tom Jones caught that *rabbit*	(He didn't catch the hare)

We have applied nothing more than simple direct emphasis in fewer than half-a-dozen examples, but by the addition of intonation and varying degrees of emphasis on more than one word, a much greater variety of meanings can be given to the sentence.

If ambiguity can arise from a printed statement as simple as this, the almost infinite variety of possibilities in Shakespeare will readily be seen. Without the exercise of imagination, the highest flights of poetic drama can be made to sound as dry as a laundry list. 'Look how the floor of heaven is thick inlaid with patines of bright gold,' is no more moving than 'Three shirts, six collars, a dozen handkerchiefs, a pair of sheets, suit of pyjamas, one table-cloth'; unless the inward image is transferred from the speaker to the listener. Lorenzo might as well say, 'Look at Portia's new carpet littered with cigarette butts.'

Variety of expression can be applied to apparently prosaic utterances. Try counting from one to twenty in some dull routine you have done a thousand times in your life before. Then imagine that on your birthday someone hands you an envelope and says, 'There's ten pounds for a present.' You put it in your pocket, 'Fine,' you say to yourself, 'that'll just pay for those L.P.s I've wanted for weeks.' On the way to buy the records, next day, you meet your best friend. He is in real trouble unless he can find ten pounds immediately. You are disappointed and at the same time eager to help. Your better nature wins; you give him the envelope and when he examines the contents, he says 'Oh no, that's too much'. You count . . . ten . . . fifteen . . . twenty! Your present was twenty pounds, not ten. You can do a good turn and also have your records. When emotion is added to routine even counting twenty can be dramatic.

Only by acute observation of spontaneous speech and action are you able to make dramatic speech and action appear natural. Human reactions are more often than not subconscious, instinctive. But the actor has foreknowledge of a dramatic situation and his response is conscious, deliberate, even contrived, although it must not appear so in the performance. The older actor after long experience, develops seemingly automatic reactions and responds effortlessly to given situations in rehearsals. This easy response to dramatic situations is part of the actor's training and is one of the reasons why repertory is so good for the young professional. Working at a different part each week provides so many opportunities in so short a time. Unfortunately, the same opportunities are denied to amateurs, who must rehearse the same parts for much longer to achieve satisfactory results.

Do not be misled by the apparent ease with which a seasoned professional actor manages a difficult part. Consider the difference between the appearance and the reality. 'Isn't he good, he's so natural,' is a typical compliment heard paid to an actor during intervals in the theatre. If he were really natural it wouldn't be a performance at all, or at least it would be a very bad one. He probably started with a natural flair for acting or he would never have taken up the theatre as a profession, though there are many people in it without talent who seem to make a living. What they must have instead is application. We know that in television the demand for performers in the comparatively new medium was so great that quality had to be sacrificed to quantity. New techniques will eventually evolve for the new medium to which the less talented will be able to apply themselves with greater diligence. The actor in repertory cannot expect the ideal part every week. He is fortunate if he is cast in a part he can 'play' one week in ten. He has to be content to 'get through' the other nine. But with a fairly sound technique, to 'get through' does not mean complete ignominy. On the contrary, he could be convincing enough in the part for the average theatre-goer and even accept-able to the more critical, who know that conditions of repertory do not allow for perfect casting.

Amateurs would do well at the beginning to realize that nothing could be further from the truth than the belief that all that is required of them is to be natural on the stage. The idea is wrongly encouraged by prefacing books on acting with Hamlet's advice to the players without an explanation of the text. When Hamlet says '. . . the purpose of playing . . . is to hold . . . the mirror up to nature . . .' (Act Three, Scene Two), Shakespeare is not advising actors to *be* natural but to *appear* natural, to *reflect* naturalness (to hold the mirror up to nature), to be as natural as the artificial conditions of the theatre allow.

If the part demands a fit of hysteria, woe betide the rest of the play, and the cast, if you take the author's directions literally. Making love is a highly personal and intimate affair. It would not be in the interests of public decency to carry it to a logical con-clusion under the glare of the spotlights in a crowded theatre. Hysteria, love scenes and murder have to be stylized to a certain extent for dramatic purposes and depend on a willing suspension of disbelief on the part of the audience for their effectiveness. What the actor does is to simulate the necessary emotional state and intensify the appearance of it to compensate for the lack of reality.

Although the actor is not being natural he must not go against the laws of nature, and even legitimate pretence should not go beyond the bounds of plausibility or good taste. There is more to it than mere credibility. A death scene can have a purifying and ennobling effect but an exhibition of violence for its own sake is degrading and sickening. There we have an extreme example of the difference between the artistic and the inartistic in the theatre. In another context but relevant to the point, G. K. Chesterton says, in a criticism of Bernard Shaw, who was a vegetarian, 'There is nothing wrong about being sick; but if Bernard Shaw wrote a play in which all the characters expressed their dislike of animal food by vomiting on the stage, I think we should be justified in saying that the thing was outside, not the laws of morality, but the framework of civilized literature.' A great deal is demanded of the actor but certain things are not expected of him and he is protected from these, first by his author and ultimately by his producer.

The greater the appearance to the audience of lack of control in a stage character, the greater must be the actual control on the part of the actor. An important thing to remember is that the ideal actor has no involuntary muscles. He must have complete control of every muscle of his body and every tone of his voice. He should be able to analyse calculatingly the vocal and physical expression of any emotion in its natural state and reproduce it in cold blood when the dramatic occasion demands, remembering the natural sequence of the components of the expression of the emotion. In the synthetic reproduction he can use a little more deliberation for dramatic effect.

In order to practise this vital self-control, do not begin with scenes or characters from plays or you will be too disappointed with the results to continue; you would have to deal with too many different things outside your own personality. Get to know yourself before you try to understand characters of someone else's creation. Imagine yourself in the simplest possible situations and coolly take note of what would be your spontaneous reactions. See whether you can reproduce every-day actions naturally. A dozen times a day you open a door or sit down or light a cigarette. Hundreds of little habitual things have become reflex actions. You do them without conscious thought or effort. But watch an inexperienced amateur doing the same things consciously on the stage at a given time in a given situation and you will be surprised at how unnatural and how laboured and self-conscious they appear. There is a lack of apparent spontaneity.

Take any simple idea which calls for a combination of voice, facial expression and gesture or movement. In spite of the simplicity it might be difficult to analyse because of the speed with which they follow each other. Briefly stated we receive an impression which transmits an idea resulting in the appropriate facial expression; this is followed quickly by a gesture or movement which in turn may be accompanied by a vocal exclamation. So that one of the first principles of dramatic technique is that facial expression precedes gesture or movement, which precedes or is accompanied by the spoken word. Of course, without the humanizing idea and emotion behind this procedure, it would be as mechanical as the actions of a marionette. We must not forget the thought which prompted the word or the action. All dramatic speech must be meaningful and any stage movement must be purposeful.

It is helpful to work to a formula of four simple words:

Think: Look: Move: Speak.

Before we go on to real dramatic exercises, take different uncomplicated situations expressing different emotions: surprise, horror, anger, despair and so on. There are no scientific rules of conduct in human situations, but for the purpose of practice, use your imagination to find examples such as the following and react to them according to the prescribed formula: Look—Move —Speak.

You are standing on the station platform and just as the train arrives, a man near you falls on the line.

You are sitting reading under a tree in a field and you are suddenly charged by a bull.

You enter a first-floor room and you greet the window-cleaner, who is outside, working. As he returns your greeting, the ladder gives a lurch and the man disappears.

You are alone, watching television, completely absorbed, when someone creeps up behind you and tickles your ribs.

You are on holiday, in Paris for the first time. You open your first letter there and learn of the death of someone you love.

If these examples sound banal, at least they evoke laughter and tears, which are elements of drama. Unless you can produce apparently spontaneous reactions after practising them over and over again you will have difficulty in responding sympathetically to the subtleties of character and situation in a play. Character drawing requires greater powers of concentration and observation than dramatic situation; you should learn to run before you try to jump.

Let us return to the bank clerk and the chairman of the bank used in an earlier example. This time imagine yourself to be the older man. Build up a little scene for yourself. The beginning has already been suggested. The end is the angry dismissal of the younger by the older man. If the incident were real he might do no more than indicate the door or tell him to get out, without moving a muscle. Neither would have any particular wish to be overheard and only two people are involved. But in a play this might be the end of a scene; at least a minor climax in an act of the play. The producer might want to 'build it up' using the action *and* the speech, intensifying both for dramatic purposes. The scene might be set with both men seated with a table between them, the younger man between the older man and the door. The bank clerk has said something which tries the patience of the other beyond endurance. The latter rises, determined to end the interview. There is a pause, absolute stillness and silence. He then crosses in front of the table and the younger man and stands resolutely between him and the door. He looks at him with an expression of hatred on his face. He then looks at the door and as he turns his head again to the younger man, raises his arm and points to the door with a determined gesture, then says, 'Get out!' He holds the position while the younger man rises and crosses in front of him to the door. The older man follows the younger one with his eyes until the door is slammed, when he is left on the stage alone. He stands motionless for a few seconds, then gradually his shoulders drop, his face sags, he takes a couple of weary steps to the chair vacated by the young man and flops into it, his head in his hands. There you have a dramatic situation worked out technically with very little material. Now try working the same scene with the sequence reversed to Speak; Move; Look: and you will have the opposite of a dramatic scene. It is no exaggeration to say that this reversal has occurred more than once on the amateur stage, only to be met with titters from the audience, not one member of which could have explained why he was amused.

Most people interested in the theatre are familiar with the cliché that the stage is larger than life. While it is true it is sometimes misunderstood and consequently worth developing. The voice requires more volume and speech greater rhythm; action is studied and movement elaborated; emotion is intensified; focus is sharper. If you are telling a story to a group of people round a fireside, your audience is near enough to you to pick up every point through subtle changes in your voice, natural inflections, pauses, emphasis in your general delivery. They are in close enough proximity to see the facial expression which accompanies any emotional change. All that is necessary is for the narrator to be sincere and natural. If he can feel it he can express it . . . but this is not so on the stage. The sincerity and emotion might be there but they are not expressed with sufficient force for them to reach the audience. The word sincerity is often misused as a theatrical term. On the stage the actor is creating, or re-creating a character, whose ideas and feelings must be projected into the

auditorium. In fact there is no creation without projection. One
might say that the character is still-born. It is no good thinking that you can do something different on the stage from
what you have done in the rehearsal rooms. Rehearsals are not
only for learning lines. Real rehearsing does not begin until you
are fairly familiar with your lines. The amount of projection
necessary for your particular auditorium has to be assessed
during the rehearsal without the actor feeling embarrassed by the
proximity of his fellow-actors. If he is self-conscious with them
he will probably be more so with the greater numbers in the
audience. If you consider the difference between rehearsal in a
small room and performance in a theatre as merely a matter of
distance—though in reality it is much more than that—you will
at least begin to realize how the disadvantage can be overcome.
Consider how far the actor is from the man in the back row of the
stalls. Don't bother about the front row until judgement has
come from experience. How does the gulf between you affect his
sight and hearing? How much of your interpretation is lost in
transferring it from you to him? You might think you are acting
your head off or tearing a passion to tatters; but the man in the
back row might think you are insipid, feeble and colourless. The
answer is, obviously, to exaggerate, but how much exaggeration
is necessary for what you do on the stage to fall naturally on the
eye and ear of the audience can only be learned from experience
and the producer. It is part of the producer's job to ensure, as
far as lies in his power, that the production will not suffer as a
result of an actor making a fool of himself on the stage. In fact,
with an amateur group, one of the first responsibilities of the
producer is to save people from themselves.

But you can rest assured that very few amateurs over-act. They
may act badly or they may not act at all, but that is a different
thing from over-acting. With one or two notable exceptions they
more often than not err on the side of under-acting and this is
to be expected bearing in mind the infrequent opportunities for
acting of the average amateur.

Considering how long it takes the professional to learn the
business, it says a great deal for the intelligence of the average
amateur that the best of their work will stand up to serious
criticism. It is only the hard-boiled professionals, and then only
the undisciplined ones, who over-act. They are the 'ham' actors
who have lost all sense of proportion and observation. They live

in a world of make-believe where nothing exists except 'lines' and 'business'. They live only when they face an audience, spot-lighted centre-stage. One is reminded of a chorus-girl past her best and her extravagant use of make-up. As time goes on she is relegated from the front to the back row of the chorus. To compensate she reddens her lips and blues her eyes until she becomes sub-human and looks like a parrot. But such people are not of anybody's world but their own. Forget about them.

Before going on to more detailed exercises and the practice of technique, let us sum up the general remarks of this introduction to acting.

Do everything you have to do on the stage with a singleness of purpose. Whatever you have to do, do it deliberately or not at all. Don't do anything apologetically; never make half-hearted movements or indecisive speeches on the stage. Such things only embarrass your audience. Your confidence is reflected in the audience and puts them at their ease. Don't confuse lack of confidence with modesty; on the other hand don't mistake a thick skin and sickening affectations for self-confidence. The secret is self-control. When you have complete control of your voice and body and can make them react to a given situation exactly as you wish; when you have brought mental flexibility and physical agility to an art and can command a state of tension or relaxation at will; when you have learned the value of repose and can carry the audience with you in all your various simulated moods and conditions—you can claim to have mastered dramatic technique. But don't think you can do it all by reading this or any other book.

*　　　*　　　*

Up to the present we have been dealing with the external aspects of acting; the barest requirements of technique or the parts of the craft which to some extent can be taught. Every painter learns the principles of draughtsmanship just as every musician must know harmony and counterpoint, but irrespective of these rudiments there are the imponderables which are difficult enough to discuss, and probably impossible to teach. The true artist is perhaps only half aware of the qualities he possesses which lift him out of the sphere of run-of-the-mill craftsmen into the realm of artistry. The critic can do no more than analyse and assess results or performance.

The actor has been denied admission to the category of the artist by many critics. For the purpose of argument we can allow him the rank of interpretive, if not creative, artist, as we do the concert pianist. We are not dealing here with genius, which is beyond our understanding; at the same time we should not forget the dictum that 'genius is an infinite capacity for taking pains'. The work of great painters, composers and writers can be judged by posterity after their deaths. The work of a great actor dies—not with him only—but with each performance. No one would question that Shakespeare was the greatest writer in the English-speaking world but no one can prove that Garrick, Irving or Bernhardt were greater actors than Gielgud, Olivier or Edith Evans. The actor has little evidence of the traditions of acting on which to draw despite the research of scholars, one of whom was misguided enough to 'demonstrate' the speech of the Elizabethan actor on the radio, when he was incapable of mastering the technique of contemporary speech for the medium he was using!

That actors are born and not made is a half-truth. Certainly anyone without a natural flair for acting could never become any more than a competent technician with the best teaching in the world and, incidentally, there would be no theatrical profession without such people. On the other hand anyone who believes that all that is required of him is natural talent will fall by the way-side—and probably earlier than the trained actor without talent! Witness the crop of infant prodigies who never develop into mature actors. The most striking example is the Young Roscius, or Master William Betty. At the start of the nineteenth century he was the rage of Covent Garden and Drury Lane after con-quering audiences in Scotland and Ireland. His performances of the great Shakespearean roles were preferred to those of Kemble and Mrs Siddons for a time. On one occasion the House of Commons was adjourned to enable the younger Pitt to see his Hamlet. He was about thirteen at the time and it was not long before he fell out of favour. In his early twenties, after going to Cambridge, he tried to make a come-back on the stage but was a dismal failure. He died in complete obscurity when he was over eighty. The Dublin Roscius, Brooke, followed him a few years later. His success at the age of fourteen was phenomenal, but his later career was mediocre. Yet the original Roscius, a contem-porary of Cicero and the most famous of Roman actors, is said to have owed his success to painstaking study, thinking out and practising every gesture before trying it out in performance.

The biographies of all great actors show that constant practice, attention to detail and attempts at improvement and experiment at every stage of their careers, are essential for keeping the art of the actor alive and fresh and true to life.

Naturally, what the great actors have to say about acting must be of tremendous interest for the amateur though he will be disappointed if he expects any of them to divulge a secret formula, or, for that matter, information which might be of immediate benefit to his acting. On the one hand there appears to be general agreement about ends, and on the other controversy and even contradiction as to means. Which provides the better results, inspiration or deliberation? Should emotion on the stage be real or simulated? Is intelligence or sensibility the more important qualification for the actor? These are questions unanimous answers to which the student-actor will search for in vain! He will choose those with which he is already in sympathy by reason of temperament. One can only echo a cry of the eighteenth century from Colley Cibber's *Apology for his Life* '. . . What talents shall we say infallibly form an actor? This, I confess, is one of nature's secrets, too deep for me to dive into . . .' Or quote the great French actor, Talma, 'Between two persons destined for the stage, one possessing extreme sensibility and the other a profound intelligence, I would without question prefer the former . . . If the actor is not endowed with a sensibility at least equal to that of any of his audience he can move them but very little. It is only by an excess of sensibility that he can succeed in producing deep impressions and move even the coldest souls. The power that raises must be greater than the power raised.'[1] But one might add, with due humility, that though sensibility may be the better qualification for a tragic role, perhaps intelligence should take precedence in high comedy. The emotional appeal will provoke tears; laughter is nearer the intellectual plane. Audiences are more easily moved by the sincerity of schoolboys in Shakespearean tragedy than they are amused, except by their *gaucherie*, in a comedy of manners.

All actors agree on the necessity of technique of some kind, though they may differ about method or application. A celebrated controversy between Irving and Coquelin, the French actor who

[1] *Actors On Acting;* Cole and Chinoy.

first played Cyrano de Bergerac, brought comment from all and sundry, including Salvini, the Italian whose Othello was said at the time to be the greatest of all. Coquelin claimed that it was not necessary for an actor to feel personally the emotion he hoped to produce in his audience through the medium of the character in the play. The actor, he said, must have a dual personality; his first self—the actor, and his second self—the instrument. The first works on the second to produce a work of art with every character that is played. The actor is the artist who subjects the instrument to his will. The first is the master with the second always subservient; the more absolute the subjection the greater the artist, or actor, who must never let the part 'run away' with him. 'Whether your second self weeps or laughs, whether you become frenzied to madness or suffer the pains of death, it must always be under the watchful eye of your ever impassive self, and within certain fixed and prescribed bounds.' [1]

The argument is the old one of heart and head. But the difference of opinion was one of degree and not of kind. Irving did not recommend that actors should allow themselves to be carried away by their feelings; he said that nothing could be more erroneous than the belief that great actors trust to the inspiration of the moment. Both he and Salvini would re-create the emotion, or foster the illusion of the first experience of the character, whenever possible. They were indignant with Coquelin for his cold-blooded approach to characterization and his calculated method for the simulation of emotion. The difference is one of identification with, or representation of, the character.

No serious book on acting could disregard Stanislavski, whose influence has been greater than that of any individual on the theatre of the twentieth century. What is today known as 'The Method' is a simplification—unless 'modification' or 'elaboration' are kinder words—of the system of training worked out by Constantin Stanislavski at the Moscow Arts Theatre from its inception just before the turn of the century. There is nothing simple and there are no short cuts to acting in Stanislavski's system. To read his books requires patience and concentration and to apply his methods demands nothing short of dedication. But the reward is worth the effort for anyone who is prepared to read and re-read—if he can understand them.

Stanislavski did not invent a grammar of acting. Others before

[1] Ibid.

him had expressed opinions and propounded theories: Diderot, for instance, in France in the eighteenth century who argued against sensibility. Stanislavski was the first to record systematically the internal as well as the external development of the true actor from A to Z. Hard-bitten middle-aged actors who were introduced to his books would probably declare them romantic or melodramatic. New worlds are open to the young who come to him with faith, imagination and intelligence. I once mentioned his book *An Actor Prepares* to a professional producer, who said impatiently, 'But that's only what every professional actor knows'. I replied politely, 'That's what I want my amateur actors to know,' but thought, 'He hasn't read it, or if he has, he doesn't understand it.'

Stanislavski found the contemporary theatre hamstrung by the conventions and trappings accumulated by several generations of actors. He wanted to substitute artistic truth for artificial theatricality. A new technique was required for the new drama, Tchekhov, for example. Bombast gave place to naturalism. Ibsen was on the way in; the grandiose had to give way to acquired sincerity and simplicity. Instead of external embellishment Stanislavski demanded inner conviction. He claimed that acting was a creative and not a representational art. A professional actor remarked to me recently, 'There is no such thing as dramatic art, there is only stage trickery.' Such an attitude may be satisfactory to the professional careerist or the amateur exhibitionist but the devoted amateur will seek for something more. It was against tricks and mannerisms and outward show that Stanislavski argued. Form matters less than content. He was more interested in soul than in structure. The world is not deceived with ornament for long.

The Stanislavski system demands a greater depth of human understanding than is required for some of its more superficial imitations. You can *act* an inanimate object or one of the lower animals but you cannot *be* one. You can ask a child to pretend to be a cash register or a frog; you insult an adult by asking him to do likewise, unless he has the mentality of a child—or a frog! You cannot expect a child to give a demonstration of unbridled emotion at will, nor can you expect an adult to do so. The best you will be given is a demonstration of a demonstration, without the emotion. It will not be acting but charades. Emotion has to be experienced internally, not shown externally, in order to be transferred. It is the transference which matters, not the showing. But the emotion of the actor must have gone through a refining process; the original, minus the shock to the nervous system, and none the less moving for not being raw. The purpose of acting is to move without shock. The actor's emotion is relived feeling, controlled by thought and transferred by technique.

Stanislavski has a chapter on 'Emotion Memory'. This is a different thing from factual memory, remembering dates, figures and details or being a 'good study'—being able to memorize your lines quickly. It is possible to have a bad factual memory and a good emotion memory, or vice versa. To be able to remember emotions associated with an incident, even if one forgets the details of the cause of the emotion, is advantageous to the artistic development of the actor. Emotion memory can be cultivated to a certain extent in the same way as imagination and the earlier the age the practice is started the more successful it will be. A considerable amount of the actor's capital, and nearly all his reserves, are stored in his subconscious mind. His power of recall from the subconscious to the conscious depends upon his capability for subjective observation of true emotion in real life. An actor can use his subconscious as an industrialist uses 'time and motion', for economy of wear and tear. Without the application of the principle of emotion memory he runs the risk of becoming either a mechanical actor or a neurotic.

It is the subconscious that provides inspiration—which is not to be ruled out of the actor's art. The more inspiration the finer the artist, but it cannot be relied on, being only in a small degree the result of preparation and for the greater part accident. No performance can be wholly inspired. Inspiration comes in flashes, momentarily, very often as a surprise to the actor and more often without his knowledge of it having happened. You cannot control the subconscious, you can only feed it. That of the younger actor will, naturally, not be as well supplied as that of the mature actor who has carefully nourished it from years of emotional experience. The student actor relies on natural talent and simple sincerity while working towards technique, acquired sincerity and experience.

Direct quotation from the life-work of Stanislavski would be invidious. His books must be interpreted by each individual according to his own temperament. I believe an actor would be the poorer for not having read *An Actor Prepares* and *Building a*

Character. Suffice it to say that the actor who cannot relax cannot learn, for without relaxation there can be no release of emotion. There can be no drawing upon the accidentals or auxiliaries of the subconscious, inspiration or intuition, unless there is a sound basis of technique. In his most violent passion the actor must be able to observe and control himself and his audience. In this context the Greek actress, Paxinou, referred to 'the third eye' in a 'Monitor' television interview with Huw Wheldon, i.e. while she and the audience are watching each other, she is also watching herself critically.

Perhaps the nearest approach to application of the Stanislavski system was in the productions of The Group Theatre in the U.S.A., which was founded just before the Second World War. The Group Theatre worked on the ensemble plan without which Stanislavski's principles cannot operate successfully. The system requires complete involvement and sympathy of every individual member of the theatre, each one knowing and understanding the work and personalities of the others. (It would be ideal for an amateur group consisting of young people prepared to sacrifice the social side to the acting end, with a producer of imagination who was prepared for experiment, all of whom could work together for a long period.) The Group Theatre brought Stella Adler's production of Clifford Odet's *Golden Boy* to London. It was a theatrical experience to be remembered long after dozens of more stereotyped presentations of much greater plays are forgotten. A simple story, verging on the melodramatic, moved and enthralled audiences by the sheer power of the acting and direction—if they ever thought of the latter. A young violinist decides to become a boxer to provide money for his poor family. His hands are ruined, he can no longer play the violin and he destroys his soul. It was inspiring and a privilege to see.

The most successful results in 'method' acting have been in films, a medium in which naturalistic acting is both suitable and effective. In the cinema, intimacy, or at least proximity, can more easily be suggested by mechanical means. Except in a synthetic way, no actor-audience relationship exists. The actor does not have to project himself, he is projected artificially by the mag-nification of his image on the screen and the amplification of his voice on the sound track. In the theatre, audience participation is vital to the actor, even though it is mute and the actor must project his emotions through speech and action to meet the audience half-way.

Herein lies part of the basic difference between acting for film and stage and the beginner must not be misled into believing he can imitate successfully in the theatre what actors appear to do on the screen. The uninitiated may think that emotions and actions are larger than life in the film; they were probably smaller, within a narrower acting range, in the studio, especially in intimate scenes and close-ups.

Anyone who is old enough to remember films such as *Rebel Without a Cause* with James Dean or *On the Waterfront* in which Marlon Brando gave a performance which made screen history, has seen 'method' acting at its best. In the latter Brando has a duologue with his gangster brother in a taxi, mostly in semi-close-up. Although the brother does all the talking it is Brando's reactions which make the scene memorable. With little more than implacable facial expression, an occasional grunt or inarticulate noise and a shake of the head, he gives a performance of poignant beauty unrivalled in the annals of the cinema.

Granted Brando's superb artistry, the same scene would hardly have registered in the theatre if it had been acted in the same way—unless to the front row in an intimate or arena theatre. It is a good test of critical faculty to observe Brando in a different kind of part in the same medium—a part which demands the technique of voice and speech. Listen to the gramophone record of the sound track of *Julius Caesar* in which Brando plays Antony. You will be surprised, to say the least, and you will have learned something. Bear this in mind when the producer says 'But it's not your part' when you are convinced that you can play the character, remembering that Marlon Brando is a brilliant actor—in parts for which he is suited!

A good actor is a good actor in any medium and the differences of techniques for the various media are not as great as is sometimes claimed. They are differences of degree rather than of kind but they can be misunderstood by the beginner. Television is more intimate, grouping and positioning is tighter and any striving for effect or unconcealed technique is immediately apparent even to the inexpert viewer. Untrained actors occasionally meet with a modicum of success on television when there would be less hope for them on the stage. Conversely, a doyenne of the English theatre gave a television performance which was embarrassing in its theatricality. She used too much emphasis and inflection in her speech, her movements were too broad and too fussy and her facial gymnastics altogether too much for the little screen. Apparently her producer had been unable to control her and she was probably too old to modify her technique for a medium which was new to her. She remains no less an artist in the theatre.

Film, television and radio all have recourse to the microphone, which, though it is a good detector of faults, is accommodating in taking a great deal of the strain from the actor. There is, in fact, a limit to the range of voice you can use for microphone work, especially at close range. An actor used to the stage, coming for the first time to the microphone, sometimes has difficulty in adapting himself to the limitations of studio work but most find it easier once they have mastered the simpler techniques. The enunciation of the stage actor is often too positive for the microphone and he has to adopt what appears to him, by comparison, a slovenly delivery. He realizes eventually that this impression is only partly true and that some of his work is taken over by the engineers and technicians.

It is for this reason that the microphone is mentioned in a book intended for beginners in the theatre, so that they will realize that what comes out of the machine is not necessarily what goes in. Acting in the theatre is undoubtedly harder work and requires more disciplined preparation and technique from the actor. Even at the lowest level, the physical effort is more demanding in diaphragmatic effort and articulatory energy alone.

So, as a last word in this general survey—before you go on to the more detailed sections on acting—do your observation of the actor's craft *in the theatre*. Make a special effort to attend solo performances. An artist who is engaged to hold an audience by himself for a whole evening has proved himself a master. You can no longer, alas, see Ruth Draper, but in the year ending as I write it has been possible to see Gielgud in *The Seven Ages of Man*, Micheál MacLiammóir in *The Importance of Being Oscar*, and Marcel Marceau, the incomparable mime. No book could equal the instruction nor the combined courses of all the drama schools offer three such valuable lessons on speech and movement.

CHAPTER TWO

Producing the play

Iᴛ has been said that a 'producer's theatre' is not a good theatre. There is some justification for this point of view when the producer distorts his author's material and uses his actors as puppets to satisfy his own egocentric ends. In a case of this kind a play is no more than an excuse for a 'production' and there have been many such examples, especially with Shakespeare, in recent years. Every caprice and whim of the producer is indulged for the sake of novelty or change. Familiarity has bred contempt or he is bored with the old bard. He forgets that very few people see the same Shakespearean play more than twice in a lifetime and that the immortal lines may have a freshness to the audience which has been lost to him. He uses every 'gimmick' he knows to arrest the visual attention of the audience and tries to close their ears to the words with counter attractions of sound in the form of incidental music, noises off, irrelevant interpolations in the dialogue and so forth.

The omnipotence of the producer is a comparatively recent development, indeed the function of the producer himself is fairly new. The term as applied to the person responsible for interpretation and presentation originated approximately a century ago. The power of the producer increased as the conditions of the theatre changed. Theatres became larger, stage machinery more complicated. Lighting by gas brought not only greater contrivance of stagecraft but the easier control of illumination which in turn resulted in the separation of stage and auditorium; the latter could be lighted independently, allowing the curtain to be dropped for changes of scenery. The proscenium arch became a picture frame for changing pictures. Audiences came to expect more and more novelty and detail in stage mechanics, properties, furniture and scenery. This was part of the birth of realism in the theatre, the demands of which now went beyond mere acting alone. The various elements of presentation required a co-ordinating hand. The producer came into being.

There are older actors, even today, who claim that the producer is superfluous, but bearing in mind the different and varying facets of modern theatre it is difficult to support this view. Even the actor-manager who preceded the present-day producer was himself a producer of sorts and was largely dependent on his stage-manager for presentation. Previously the actors were subservient to the 'star' actor who could not be expected to see the relative importance of the various actors in the play to the same extent as a modern producer, who usually does not appear on the stage.

The designation given in America to the person we call the producer is a better description, and certainly more accurate. There the producer finances the enterprise. The person who directs the play is, simply, the director, a term now coming more and more into use in the English theatre.

Whatever the merits or demerits of the office in the professional theatre, and whether it is one of producer, director or even *régisseur*, it is an absolutely indispensable one in the amateur theatre. With the best will in the world, no amateur can be expected to give the same singleness of mind to the theatre as should the professional actor or producer. He would be either foolish or fanatical who neglected his means of livelihood for his hobby. For the reason alone that it is only a relaxation from real work and at most a secondary interest to amateurs, responsibility for presenting a play must be shared. There must be one person who produces and others who act, apart from the other onerous offices in any amateur dramatic production. Anyone who attempts the double task of acting and production can hardly avoid sacrificing one to the other.

By comparison with the amateur producer, the professional producer has a fairly light task (though he may claim greater responsibility). He is dealing with professionals, both actors and technicians, all of them trained in the theatre and familiar with the terminology. The amateur producer is more often than not dealing with raw material, very often of both actors and stage-management. He must be able, not only to direct, but to teach the rudiments. Examples of the blind leading the blind will immediately spring to mind, where neither actors nor producer know anything about their craft.

The amateur producer must accept responsibility for the success or failure of the production and consequently must assume absolute control. After reading the play he will decide on the interpretation and its artistic presentation. It must be understood at the beginning that all other non-acting officers are really only his deputies and he should be able to take over the duties of any one of them in the kind of emergency which so often arises in amateur production. The producer will naturally not be as expert with the sewing machine as his wardrobe mistress; as proficient with paint and brush as his scenic artist; or as practised with hammer and saw as his carpenter. But he will at least have an eye for line, colour and form and what is more important, he knows what he wants. He will also have learned what it is difficult to tell the seamstress, painter or joiner, who have been persuaded to come into the amateur theatre on the strength of his or her particular skill. That is, that the detail and finish necessary for examination and close scrutiny are not necessary in the theatre, at least not in the amateur theatre where time is at a premium. This is not applicable to things of a practical nature. Obviously, a door or a window which has to open and close, must be absolutely fool-proof. The same should be said of stage effects and noises off, and a practical light switch on-stage must work. But a great deal of time is sometimes sacrificed to the pride of the craftsman who insists on the final polish he would give to an exhibit which is to be scrutinized at close quarters, back, front, sideways, upside-down and inside out, by a critical examiner. There is a great deal of illusion in the theatre. An artist who has a sense of perspective and a feeling for line, colour and form will paint a better backcloth or cut-out by using a broad, bold sweep of the brush than one who sees the work simply as an enlargement of a picture he is exhibiting in the local art exhibition. The same argument could be used about costume. Minute detail, however superb, can be lost on an audience, very few of whom come to the theatre armed with binoculars. This is not to say that cheap material or shoddy workmanship can ever be tolerated in the theatre. It does mean, however, that no producer has ever brought in a building contractor to construct a set with bricks and mortar for nine-inch cavity walls because the author stipulated Mr So-and-so's Drawing Room with french window at back, fireplace right, and door left, leading into hall. If there ever has been such a producer, he has missed his vocation and should have been an architect—but on second thoughts, he would have been too lacking in imagination to excel in this profession either.

The actual duties of the amateur producer are harder to define than are those of the professional producer with his hordes of minions, all of them qualified practitioners in their own field. One cannot imagine any producer, however eminent, saying to Oliver Messel or Sean Kenny, 'Could you lift this here?' or 'Sink that there,' or 'Do you think the proportions are right for that depth of skyline?' but the amateur producer may have to say 'Sparks can't provide the lighting I asked for, it'll have to be directional on the fireplace after all. Could you give me something firmer to take it?' or 'We can't have the window at the back now. We find we must have the blank wall there so that we can store the furniture for Act Two. Smith's have sent us a bigger suite than the one they promised. The window will now be stage-right, which upsets the lighting plot. Would you mind altering your shadows and highlights in the set for Act One?'

The producer will on occasion have to compromise and even to some extent sacrifice principles in order to preserve the personal relations without which no amateur production can be successful. On one occasion the set required an elegant hall of an old manor house. An atmosphere of age and antiquity was essential. The producer thought himself fortunate in having a designer whose ideas on construction were excellent. Unfortunately, his feeling for atmosphere was not of the same standard. The set was prepared, with panelled walls and a magnificent staircase, alcoves and sunken recesses, giving a remarkable effect of depth and solidity. The producer congratulated everyone concerned. All that was left to be done was the painting, which couldn't be completed until a day or so before the dress-rehearsal. When, finally, the producer was invited by the designer to approve of the finished product his enthusiasm was so dampened that he was momentarily unable to hide his disappointment from the designer, who had supervised the painting. The grand old hall looked as though it had been decorated only the day before, which indeed it had. The panel frames were in a bright gilt, surrounding floral decorations in all the splendour of full bloom. It was all rich and well done. How could one be critical of such good work? But it hadn't the faded glory, the look of permanence or time-lessness envisaged by the producer. In fact, by comparison with what he had expected, it was nothing short of brash. It was too late for him to cover his disappointment but he said, over-enthusiastically, that it was splendid. 'But you don't really think so, do you? You don't like it,' said the designer, who had, in truth, given a great deal of time and energy to the work. The producer summoned up his courage. 'Basically, it's magnificent,' he said, 'I think it's just a little shiny for the feeling of the play. I'd be awfully grateful if you would try doing it all over in a light wash, just to tone it down a bit, you know, to give the impression of age.' 'You think it looks vulgar,' snapped the designer. 'No! Oh no! Nothing of the kind,' said the producer, wishing now that he had not come on it so suddenly and in the presence of the designer, 'I only think it looks a bit new.' 'Then find someone else to make it look old,' retorted the angry designer. 'Oh, come,' the producer was miserable, 'you know I would never imply criticism of your work by letting anyone else even touch it.' 'Then take or leave it,' was the embittered reply. 'I'll take it, with gratitude,' said the producer in an attempt at conciliation. Later, he sought out his lighting operator and asked him if he would modify the lighting plot. 'But you haven't tried it yet with the costumes and set,' protested Sparks. 'What in blazes *do* you want?' 'I want you to take out all the over-head batten lighting and replace any spotlights set at an angle by shaded vertical spots. Where this isn't possible, for instance, with any front-of-house spots, angle them as low as possible for effective lighting on the actors, with the minimum of "spill" on the upright surfaces of the set. I want no direct light on the actual set and the absolute minimum of reflected light.' 'But why didn't you ask for this at the beginning?' asked Sparks, with a gesture of despair. 'Because I now think that if I can highlight the actors and sink the set, the effect will be to elicit sympathy for the characters and give the impression that they are victims of their environment,' replied the producer, lamely, but with as much confidence as he could muster. 'O.K. You're the boss,' said Sparks resignedly. It worked. The producer and designer stood at the back of the theatre on the first night. 'Well?' asked the designer jubilantly. 'It's great,' said the producer relieved and pleased. 'What did I tell you?' was the comment of the more than pleased designer. 'Yes, of course you were right, and a thousand thanks,' was all the producer had to say.

No specific rules can be laid down for amateur production. It is not yet, in this country at least, an examinable subject—and long may the present conditions continue. Nor is it an academic pursuit; it is concerned with life as experience rather than with learning. At the same time the producer must be at least literate, but by no means a book-worm. He needs red blood in his veins, not printer's ink. He should have a feeling for language but it should be the language of the spoken, not the written word. He is provided with his script. It is for him to interpret it in terms of the human condition in all its varied and fascinating manifestations. It is not for him to use the book as a dead thing to be analysed and tabulated and docketed—and certainly not 'corrected'. Nor must he imagine himself as an amateur pyschiatrist or social scientist. He takes his characters as they are presented to him, as individuals in their own little world of their particular play, not as units of the larger society. He is interested in the reasons for their particular behaviour within the limits of their short life on the stage and while he will naturally ask himself *why*, he is primarily concerned with *how* they behave and not how they *should* behave.

Perhaps the one qualification a producer cannot afford to be without is a natural liking for and curiosity about people. The misanthrope would never see a production through. Of course, there is a happy medium between the incorrigible romantic and the confirmed cynic. There are amateur producers lacking in critical faculty who take their authors too much on trust: the sentimental one will assume that the poor are all good and the rich all bad; the snobbish one believes that the rich are superior and the poor objects of ridicule. He would be inhuman who was unbiased. One is either biased or dead. The producer should not only know, but understand his prejudices so that he can give all his characters a fair crack of the whip. A good playwright will have made this easy. Shakespeare always did and for this reason he is safe for the fair-minded producer. He was always judicious without being judicial and presented human frailties without condemnation. Even his villains are given enough rope to hang themselves and Richard Crookback, in his self-condemnatory opening soliloquy, is allowed a little self-justification when he says:

> '. . . Since I cannot prove a lover,
> To entertain these fair well-spoken days,
> I am determined to prove a villain,
> And hate the idle pleasures of these days.'

And on whose side is Shakespeare in *Richard the Second*? Richard's or Bolingbroke's? One of the tests of a good play is the capacity of the author for compassion. He must not be muddle-headed. The issue can be clear-cut and the characters well-defined without being black and white. Joan, in Shaw's play, commands our sympathy, but The Inquisitor, who condemns her, arouses our admiration. We may be horrified at the murder of Becket as presented by T. S. Eliot but we cannot but respond to the loyalty, even though misplaced, of the Knights.

Was Shakespeare being cynical when he made Hamlet say:

'What a piece of work is a man! how noble in reason! How infinite in faculty! in form and moving how express and admirable! in action how like an angel! in apprehension how like a god! the beauty of the world! the paragon of animals!'?

Out of its context it takes 'a bit of swallowing', admittedly. Nevertheless, the producer who starts with this as a measuring rod of humanity, even though more often than not he will be tempted to steal a glance at the next lines . . .

'And yet to me, what is this quintessence of dust?
Man delights not me; no, nor woman neither.'

will, in the long run, get the best out of the play—and his actors.

Reading the Play

There is a great deal of difference between a book and a dramatic production. The printed copy of the play is no more theatre than a score of music is an orchestral concert. There are intelligent people who enjoy reading novels who admit that they are almost incapable of reading a play. On the other hand, just as there are a few people who claim to be able to 'hear' music by reading the score, there are those who prefer the script of a play to the performance of it in a theatre. They must have enviable and vivid imaginations. Or they have probably seen a bad production which ruined their original conception of a favourite play. Again, it may simply be that they have no sense of theatre. But the fact remains that plays are written to be acted and not for silent reading.

No less a theatrical producer and scholar than Nevill Coghill has said, 'Anyone with experience of producing plays will have known how difficult it is to hear and visualize a play before he stages it. He knows that before he stages it he must be able to discern the idea that governs and gives it unity, and then to imagine the décor, the lighting, the costumes, the movement, the gestures and tones of voice that will subserve this governing idea in every detail of the play. All that wealth of meaning has to be co-ordinated, and in doing so one may be involved in weeks of research and judgement. And it is a fact that even then, when the producer has imagined the play as devotedly as he knows how, he finds that on coming into rehearsal he has missed meanings which only rehearsal can bring forth.'

The immense difference between the power of the spoken word and that of the written word in drama can be appreciated only through interpretation and performance. Anyone who doubts this has only to read the script of *Waiting for Godot*, which is almost incomprehensible to the average reader, and then to witness the revelation of meaning in the theatrical performance of the same play. It is a demonstration of the difference between the skeleton or bare statement of literary language and the full implication of idea and the interplay of character through speech. The ultimate purpose of the drama, even as entertainment, is the appreciation and comprehension of human qualities and situations. And what better medium can we have for this purpose than human beings on the stage?

So the producer must have aural and visual imagination. When he reads dramatic dialogue he must be able to 'hear' people talking as well as 'see' what they are doing and how each of them reacts to what the others have to say. Each 'speaker' will take on individual characteristics, even of voice and mannerisms. The producer will be aware of the location and note whether it is familiar or alien to the several characters. He will know from what he 'hears' and 'sees', while he is reading, the natural environment of each of them. He will identify himself, not only with one of the characters, but with each one in turn and he will try to imagine what the rest are thinking while one is speaking.

No producer will be able to do this at one reading. He should read and re-read the play until he has as clear a picture in his mind of all the characters and their motives as he has of himself and his own. Not until he has done this should he think of holding a reading for casting.

The Producer and the Actor

When the producer turns to the association of his actors with the play under consideration he should approach the question of

acting simply. Far too many young actors have been discouraged
by 'isms' and 'osms' and pseudo-intellectual attitudes. Psychological explanations of the desire to act are questionable. The
impulse to act or play in public is as natural as wanting to play
tennis or bridge and is older than either. It is sufficient that young
people want to do it. The false bohemianism and 'arty' atmosphere common to the less desirable dramatic societies as often
as not emanate from the attitudinizing of producers. Amateur
acting can be as healthy, relaxing or stimulating as any other
activity.

Before literacy became universal, with the comparatively recent
emergence of the novel, play-acting was a popular form of story-
telling. With the passage of time it has, of course, acquired certain
formalities and conventions. But even now, when a play is
produced, it is still, essentially, no more than a matter of a small
group of people telling a story to a larger group of people; a
story in sound, movement and animated three-dimensional
pictures. It is the analysis of these three basic elements which the
drama producer studies for the preparation of his play. Once the
producer has recognized these elementary principles he can start
with technical analysis and work up to artistic synthesis. All art
is subject to form but the difficulty lies in seeing the parts which
make up the whole.

The most important part is, obviously, that of the actors who
have to tell the story. One actor cannot tell the whole of the story.
Each has to tell part of it through the particular character he or
she is playing, but it must flow as if it were being told by a single
narrator. The actors are members of a team with varying degrees
of responsibility, but unless the producer can assess the amount
of responsibility and convey this to each of his actors, the production will naturally lack the balance without which any dramatic
production will be a failure. There is a familiar cliché, 'There are
no small parts, there are only small actors,' which like so many
clichés is only half-true. No 'bit-part' actor can be made to feel
that he is as important to the success of the play as the leading
man. But it must be impressed upon every member of the cast
that when an actor is on the stage, he is there for a specific reason
and with a definite purpose. He has to co-operate with the other
members of the team and let the one who has part of the story to
tell at a particular time have the stage to the best advantage. He
has to be seen all of the time, even if it is only for his reaction to

what someone else has to say, and he has to be seen and heard when it is his turn to speak.

When the actor has been made aware of his duty towards his fellow actors, it is for the producer to make him aware also of his duty to the audience. The people in the front are there for a particular reason too. Amateurs very often find themselves in a dilemma. Everything appears to go well at rehearsal but it seems to fall to pieces in performance. The actors were not prepared for this peculiar dichotomy or the producer was unaware of his dual function. The producer has missed the whole point of his preparation if he forgets about the audience during rehearsals. Far too often the producer is to be seen sitting in with the actors on the set. It may be necessary for detailed instructions, for demonstration of intricate bits which require repetition but he must, for a great deal of the time leave it alone, get as far away from the set as the most remote member of the audience. He should get outside of it. He must be the audience at some rehearsals even though he has to be the actors at others.

The audience is the larger group which has come to hear the story which the smaller group has to tell. Without the audience there is no performance. Often the smaller group assumes that the larger group knows the story as well as they themselves do. The producer should be constantly reminding himself when he is *being* the audience that the real audience will be seeing the production for the first time. They must see and hear the actors all the time. If the actors can't be seen by all the audience all the time, because of the producer's failure to gauge 'lines of sight' from every seat in the auditorium—through the actors standing in front of each other or by bad grouping—it is rather like looking at a picture in which the artist has gone to a great deal of trouble to paint one figure and then absent-mindedly painted another one over it. If the actors can't be seen, through bad lighting or the producer's inability to co-ordinate acting area lights and actor's position, it is as though he were to show his friends his holiday snapshot album—in the dark. If one actor can't be heard throughout the play it is worse still, like trying to read a novel with pages missing here and there. Even if only occasional words are lost it is as bad as reading a badly-printed book. The reader can at least take the book at his own speed or even turn back. With a book the reader is in control but the audience is completely at the mercy of the people on the stage. A member of the audience

would be perfectly justified if he stood up in the middle of a
performance and shouted, 'Go over the last five minutes again, I
didn't hear a word and I have completely lost the thread of the
story.'

Preparation and Casting

After reading the play several times, the producer will not start
into actual production immediately unless forced by circumstances to do so. He will give himself time for cogitation. There
are always several approaches to any production. The best one
is that which will serve the author most faithfully. What is he
saying? How best can the producer use the resources available
to bring out the inner meaning? How to distribute the parts to
heighten the conflict? Which voices to use to provide harmony
and contrast? Before he has a casting reading he must have a
clear idea how he would like to interpret the play. He will start
with a plan but not with an inflexible blue-print. He starts off with
the ideal but as likely as not, as has been said earlier, he may have
to fall back on compromise. He has the human factor to contend
with. There is no perfection in the amateur drama; there is only
artistic endeavour. To do the best with the material at hand—no
more can be asked of any producer.

In his own mind the producer knows what kind of people the
characters in the play are; but where to find them? Not in his
group; they never are! He tries the next best thing. He is not so
insensitive as to tell the actors who offer themselves for casting
his exact conceptions of the parts. Various members of the group
will be invited to read, not, as is sometimes cruelly done, half a
page, but at least a little scene complete in itself. Or better still,
if time allows, as many readings of the complete play as possible
with the same actor reading the same part throughout. If this
isn't possible apply the same principle to one act of the play.

See what the actors have to give before trying to superimpose
what the producer wants. There will never be complete affinity
and the producer will have to be content with the actor who gives
the reading which is nearest to his original idea of the character.
The two interpretations will grow nearer through discussion,
sympathy, understanding and encouragement. The onus here is
on the producer, unless he has mistakenly chosen a particularly
selfish actor.

If the producer is working with a cast for the first time he must beware of the pitfalls of a first reading and not mistake a good sight-reader for a good actor. Many excellent actors are very bad sight-readers and many good readers cannot improve on a first reading. Reading is not acting any more than acting is reading. It has to be estimated whether the good reader has possibilities of development. Sensibility and intelligence are not synonymous, and they are difficult to distinguish on first acquaintance with a person. Naturally one cannot penalize anyone for being a good reader. It may be the result of experience and he may be the better actor for being able to exercise control. One way of trying him out further is to find out whether he is 'produceable'. Has he a good ear? Can he give the character a slightly different slant in his second reading? With a halting reader the producer should be on the look-out for qualities of voice. Is it tuneful, resonant? Is the delivery basically harsh and jerky or are there indications of pleasant speech rhythms obscured by nerves? Try to get him into conversation on ground which is familiar to him so that he is less self-conscious. If he has qualities necessary to the part being considered he should not be discarded on the first poor reading.

If the reading is nowhere near to what the producer had in mind he should think twice before committing himself irrevocably to the production of that particular play.

Any producer who is determined to produce a play because he likes it, in spite of unsuitable casting, or one who allows someone else's choice of play to be thrust on him against his better judgement, deserves the consequences.

Although the producer is the final arbiter in casting and will listen to suggestions, he should bear in mind that the success of the production depends almost entirely on having the right people in the right parts. This is the most delicate part of the process of birth of a production and must not be rushed to give the appearance of being business-like or of a producer who gets on with the job.

When choice of play and casting have been decided satisfactorily the producer's task has been lightened considerably.

Planning the Rehearsals

It is important that the cast should know in advance what is expected of them, especially with regard to time. Apart from knowing when they will be required, for how long and what sections of the play they will be doing, the producer should be able to tell them in advance, roughly, the several stages of production he expects to have reached at given times, from first rehearsal to dress rehearsal. If the play has three acts and the time for preparation six weeks, he could say that he wanted Act One ready for 'run-through' on the prompt at the end of a fortnight, the same for Act Two at the end of three weeks and Act Three at the end of the month, working entirely on the prompt without books for the last fortnight. Once he has made this decision, the actor who is not ready will have to abide by it even if he has to repeat every line after the prompter. Six weeks is only a suggestion and must not be taken too literally.

A clear distinction must be made between rehearsals for direction or interpretation, and the uninterrupted run-through for continuity, of the whole or part of the play. The whole cast should know before they come to rehearsal whether it is to be intensive, with repetition for improvement and if a large group, a duologue or a single actor will be rehearsed. It is impossible to keep the whole of the cast actively engaged all the time. A certain amount of 'hanging around' is almost inevitable in the best organized dramatic societies but even the most enthusiastic actors are demoralized by too much of it. The producer should be definite about time and set an example himself if he expects punctuality from the actors.

Ideally, amateur actors require more time for rehearsal than professionals. This appears too obvious for mention except for the paradox that they usually actually have less than professionals in a West End production even if they have more than repertory actors. How can they reconcile themselves to this apparently ridiculous state of affairs? A producer touring a Shakespearean repertory company is said to have claimed two hundred hours for rehearsal of a play—with actors evidently familiar with the script. This is enough to discourage the most ardent amateur producer. But he should take heart. Let him assume that, for his own production to be one quarter as good as that of the company mentioned, he will require at least half of the time. *One hundred hours.* How many weeks has he for rehearsal? If it is a Shakespeare play with a large cast he will need at least eight weeks. That would be an average of twelve and a half hours a week. Rehearsals are usually more intensive towards the end than at the beginning. The actors need more time to themselves for grappling with the script in the early stages.

The producer uses the yard-stick of one hundred hours for himself, as the total number of rehearsals which *he* will be expected to attend. The number of hours and rehearsals attended by the actors will depend on the length and importance of the parts, and rehearsals can be arranged so that even the leading actors do not have to be present at every rehearsal. A producer may work out the first draft of his rehearsal time-table, as follows:

1st week:	2 three-hour general rehearsals and 1 two-hour rehearsal for principals	8 hours
2nd week:	1 four-hour general rehearsal and 2 three-hour rehearsals for principals	10 hours
3rd week:	2 three-hour general rehearsals and 1 four-hour rehearsal for principals	10 hours
4th week:	1 four-hour general rehearsal and 2 four-hour rehearsals for principals	12 hours
5th week:	2 four-hour general rehearsals and 1 four-hour rehearsal for principals	12 hours
6th week:	As for fourth week plus 1 three-hour rehearsal for stage management	15 hours
7th week:	As for fifth week plus 1 three-hour rehearsal for lighting	15 hours
8th week:	Four rehearsals as follows: (1) Run-through with repetition of weak parts and all stage management. (2) Run through with repetition of weak parts and all lighting and stage management cues. (3) Mock dress-rehearsal without make-up. (4) Complete dress-rehearsal as for performance followed by general discussion.	18 hours

Total .. 100 hours

With this time-table the producer will know whether he can proceed with rehearsals and avoid the last-minute panic which ruins so many amateur dramatic performances, when what is presented to the audience is a series of dress-rehearsals with a pale reflection of a performance on the last night. By allocating the time in advance in this way, the producer will know whether or not he can afford the time in the last week and the actors may decide that rehearsals are too intensive towards the end. The question of time should be thrashed out at the beginning. It is too late half-way through rehearsal to make alterations, except for postponement of performance which can have a very bad effect on all concerned and redounds on the producer as the person responsible. One producer will decide to have more intensive rehearsals at the beginning and slacken off towards the end: another will insist on extra time, perhaps ten weeks instead of eight, giving him an average of ten hours a week instead of twelve and a half hours. These are individual matters which can be decided only by the producer and the actors concerned.

With a modern play requiring only one set and half a dozen actors it may be possible to prepare it in less time than would be necessary for a Shakespearean production. But the producer should be on his guard against the apparent simplicity of such a play and over-confidence on the part of the actors towards it. The effort of building up illusion with colloquial material which is more familiar to an audience, may be much greater than with Shakespeare or romantic plays. Audiences are sometimes conditioned to an acceptance of the theatrical conventions associated with costume and poetic drama and even where they are not, the style of the language and strangeness of the costume will very often cover minor faults of the technique of speech and movement, which would be obvious even to the uncritical, in dress and settings of their own everyday lives. Furthermore, in drawing-room plays there are fewer actors to carry the load and the effort of sustaining the character throughout the performance is greater. In a modern play the characters are nearly always named and consequently assume a more definite identity than a single-entrance messenger in Shakespeare. There is certainly less visual appeal through movement and colour.

Take two outstanding productions of 1960. Compare the drabness of the setting and dress of Harold Pinter's *The Caretaker* with the lavish presentation of almost any production at Stratford. There are three actors in *The Caretaker* and the play is mainly a series of duologues. One forgets the greatest number of actors on the stage at any one time in such a play as *Troilus and Cressida*. In the first play one concentrates all the time on a single actor and watches his eyes, his lips, his hands and listens intently to every syllable. In the second, one is conscious for the greater part of the time of a general impression of contending factions more than of individual people. A recent Stratford production was beautiful to look at and to listen to and occasionally the action was halted and one savoured the glory of the lines, 'Time hath, my lord, a wallet at his back . . .' and pondered on the wisdom of the author. These were Trojans and Greeks, far removed from us in time and presented to us as an Elizabethan chose to see them, using language of a certain theatrical convention. Only now and again the remoteness diminished and we were conscious of a fully rounded character taking on the dimensions of flesh and blood . . . Ulysses, Cressida, Pandarus . . . If the amateur producer is forced to come to a decision between a choice of these two plays for casting, which will he choose? Neither, exclaims the cynic, but the cynic wasn't asked and the amateur producer will have just this kind of decision to make at some time, whether he likes it or not.

Details of Rehearsal

Although the producer will naturally use his own discretion with regard to detail of rehearsals, which must vary according to the kind of play chosen, a little guidance is necessary for those embarking on production for the first time. By a process of trial and error, the method best suited to the individual producer will be learned. Even the order of preference in detail, such as movement and positioning or interpretation of lines, is not generally agreed upon by experienced producers. If the play is a modern comedy with a small cast in a box set the initial approach can be more casual than for a romantic costume play with a large cast of principals and supernumeraries, with constantly changing scenes. The latter would require more actual organization for presentation before moves and lines were even reached. It would be necessary, almost from the beginning, to provide an acting area similar to that of the stage on which the play would finally be presented. But the small cast in the box set could be rehearsed for a considerable time in the home of the producer or a member of the cast, none of whom need even see the stage until the week before the production. The stage management and lighting teams

for the smaller production could work separately from the cast
for a longer period.

Positioning

The ideal, which is seldom possible, is to work on the actual
stage from the beginning, with actual entrances and exits,
furniture, properties and so forth to be used. Generally, rough
stage positions should be indicated to the actors. At the first
reading, where the actor must keep his eyes on the book, it is
sufficient to tell him that he is right or left or centre stage. It
should be made clear that right and left are from the actor's point
of view, as he faces the audience.

The producer should reserve the right to alter stage positions
and moves for a few rehearsals at least. Plans worked out in
theory can often be improved in practice. For this reason the
producer should ask the cast to mark the original, or provisional
moves, in their books in pencil only. When he has finally decided
on the positions and moves for a particular scene, which should
be as soon as possible, he can ask them to mark these in ink
according to a pre-arranged and standardized system. The
producer will have his own copy carefully marked for stage
directions and the stage manager will keep a note in the prompt
copy, so that when the prompter takes over, which again should
be as soon as possible, he will know the exact position of every
actor on the stage.

Writing out stage directions in full would be time-wasting and
tedious and abbreviations, so long as they are agreed upon, are
sufficient—L means 'actor's stage left'; R 'actor's stage right';
C 'centre stage'; UL 'up-left'; UR 'up-right'; DL 'down-left';
DR 'down-right'; XULC means 'Cross up left centre'. Although
these instructions appear simple, they have in the past led to
unnecessary argument and recriminations in the excitement of
rehearsal, especially when working for the first time without
books. The producer should establish positions in the way he
thinks best. The accompanying diagram (Fig. 1) is a help.

Such a diagram is, of course, only a rough guide to be used in
the preliminary stages of a production and some fluidity must
be allowed for observation of the sections of the stage marked
on it, even then. A producer might say 'Come down and in a
little right of left-centre' or 'Go up slightly right of dead centre',
but it would be not only confusing, but inhuman, to use all the

possible permutations of the positions marked in the diagram. Actors are not chessmen. Some of the positions would, in any case, hardly ever be used unless in exceptional circumstances, and even then only momentarily; UL and UR, for example. Extreme DC would be used only occasionally, say for a soliloquy. As the production develops, positions are thought of in relation

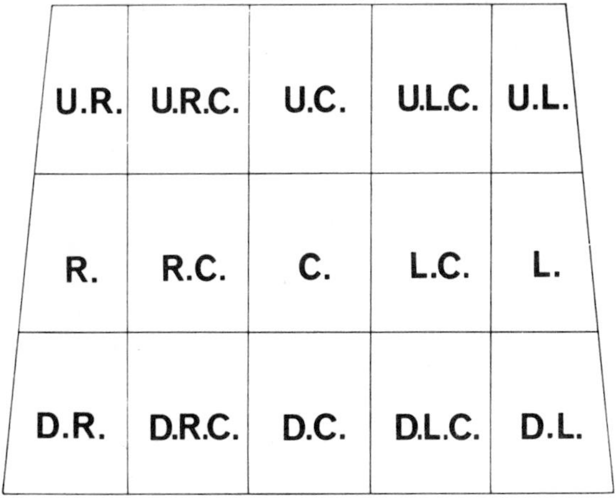

U.R.	U.R.C.	U.C.	U.L.C.	U.L.
R.	R.C.	C.	L.C.	L.
D.R.	D.R.C.	D.C.	D.L.C.	D.L.

Figure 1.

to other actors on the stage, or they are associated with scenery, a pillar, a platform, steps or items of stage furniture.

A diagram of this kind is of greater value for a large cast on an open stage with little scenery than it is for a small cast in a more realistic setting. In a drawing-room comedy or a kitchen drama there would be no point in using it at all. The scene can be set with furniture and properties in the same position for each rehearsal and simple stage directions such as 'A comes in at door UR. B is sitting reading letter left end of sofa opposite. On A's entrance B quickly hides letter under cushion right of sofa. A rushes down, seizes cushion which he throws below window UC, grabs the letter and without a word exits through the door DL. B makes for the telephone UC but falls over cushion, bringing table with telephone and contents crashing to the floor'.

Insistence on exact positions in the first few readings when an actor is struggling with his part, is only a hindrance to the development of the character. So long as he is on the correct side of the stage or of another actor it should suffice, remembering that time must be spent on details of attitude and positioning and stance when he gets rid of his book; attention to such detail would be superfluous in the early stages. The producer looks for every opportunity of saving time as well as his own and the actor's energy.

When the actors are sufficiently familiar with their scripts to keep, as it were, one eye on the set, attention can be given to greater detail and precision of movements. Lines of sight from the auditorium can easily be gauged by the producer from the extreme end seats of the front row. Amateurs are rarely fortunate enough to play in professional theatres with circle and balcony. Most of their productions are prepared in rectangular buildings for audiences at ground level with the whole of the auditorium at a lower level than that of the stage. It is unfortunate that the building is usually a multi-purpose hall, which is used for dancing, badminton or other activities of a non-theatrical kind. The producer can do nothing about the structure of his 'theatre' except to make the most of it. The tiny woman who sits behind the big broad-shouldered man in the audience is a problem which can be only slightly alleviated by 'staggering' the seats; placing them so that people can look between the heads of those in the row immediately in front of them. But everyone who can see the stage at just above its floor level can see all the actors if the two people occupying the seats at each end of the front row can see them. This applies only to the rectangular building which includes stage and auditorium. Most people are familiar with the side-seats, upstairs or down, in the professional theatre, from which only half of the action on the stage can be seen.

If there is a position in any stage-picture to which the attention of the audience is naturally drawn it is centre. But it would be very monotonous if every piece of action originated from that position. The good producer uses his actors to direct the attention of his audience to different parts of the stage at different times. There will be main and subsidiary 'acting areas', and the production must at no time be static—which is not to deny the significance of 'suspended animation'.

If two actors are on the stage, the one who is 'upstage' or

nearer to centre-back, has a natural advantage of the actor 'downstage' of him. There is the exception to every rule but the producer usually gives the dominating upstage position to the actor he wishes to impress the audience at a given time. To place the two actors parallel to the front of the stage and facing each other has the effect of neutralizing both, apart from reducing the aspect of the third dimension. Every experienced actor realizes the advantages of the upstage position. It allows him to face his audience squarely and speak directly to them, placing the other actors on the stage in a somewhat subservient position. The back of a head or even a profile cannot be as expressive as a full face, and an actor speaking into the wings or towards the backcloth cannot command the same concentration from the audience. But the actor is not a public speaker and only occasionally is he given an opportunity of speaking directly to his audience, especially in realistic plays.

The term 'upstage', with the connotation of affecting a demeanour of superiority, is now in fairly common usage and bears some relation to fact. In the old days of the visiting 'stars', and later of the actor-manager, the upstage position was claimed as a right by virtue of reputation. The stage was 'raked'; i.e. sloping downwards towards the audience. To be 'upstage' was to be at a higher level, so that the actor centre-back could tower over his fellows. The writer can remember from his childhood the old provincial 'stock' companies, in which there was little of either production or authority. It was amusing, if distracting, to watch two actors of equal demerit in contest, 'jockeying' for position. When it came to his speech each actor would 'upstage' the other and the one who arrived centre-back with his shoulder blades on the backcloth first, was the winner. Such blatant behaviour would be intolerable today but the producer must be on the lookout for trickery in performance. Occasionally the half-experienced actor will try to get the advantage of the tyro.

The producer always has in mind the dual purpose of using the positions of the actors for bringing out the meaning of the words and creating a pleasant or stimulating picture to augment the meaning, suiting the action to the word and the word to the action. Needless to say, sympathy or intimacy would seldom be suggested with one actor Down Right and another Up Left, nor would there be visual harmony in the composition of the picture; the eye would have to travel too far between the objects of

interest for the desired emotional state. Such positioning would
be more effective for the suggestion of antagonism, or opposition
of the characters, and disunity of the visual image. Generally,
separation of the characters can heighten animosity and proximity
suggest amicability. Extreme illustrations are shouted threats
and the embrace. It would be just as incongruous to have Brutus
and Cassius standing so closely that they were screaming into
each other's teeth throughout the quarrel scene as it would be for
Romeo and Juliet to address each other from opposite corners
of Juliet's chamber: yet in neither could the scene be immobile.
The producer works out a basic pattern suitable to the emotional
content, with variations on a given theme.

Movement

Stage movement is part of the development of the production.
'Moves' arise out of the content; they are motivated by the words.

Movement for its own sake is never convincing. Unless the
producer can give reasons for a move he should not insist on the
actor carrying out his direction. Action is born of situation and
the actor must be persuaded of its justification. In every play
there are alternating periods of activity and repose. There appears
to be growing tendency, even in the professional theatre, never
to allow the eyes of the audience to rest for more than a few
seconds, as though the producer had no confidence in either
author or actor to hold the interest of the audience by subject
matter or personality. Fussy movement is irritating but a big
movement following a few moments of comparative stillness can
be effectively used for dramatic emphasis, change of mood or for
working up to a minor climax. A decisive movement isolating an
individual actor from a crowd can be dramatic in itself; or the
separation of a group into protagonists may be as highly sugges-
tive of factional intentions as speech. A climax which has been
reached by quick or violent action accompanied by shouting can
be strengthened by the anti-climax of sudden statuesque quietness,
or 'holding a still'.

The movement of any single actor should be considered in
relation to the composition of the animated picture. The various
elements of the picture must be in proportion for maintaining
the unity of dramatic intention. The relative positions of the
actors, the significance of bodily attitudes, all contribute to the
general and immediate effect on the audience. Animation on the

stage is improved by depth in the setting. In spite of what has been said about the upstage position of one of two actors, or on a raked stage, an actor on a crowded stage can lose significance if he is too far back and on the same level as the actors in the foreground. If different levels can be used to raise the picture as it recedes into the background, adding the dimension of height to that of depth, greater dominance is afforded the actor.

The application of the principles, positions and moves mentioned in the preceding paragraphs is more or less limited to the non-realistic play on an open stage. In a domestic play with a box set, opportunities for imaginative movement do not arise to the same extent. But even in the drawing-room comedy an observant producer can avoid dull composition of picture by avoiding the monotony of parallel lines in either a vertical or horizontal direction. It is uninspiring, to say the least, to have all the actors sitting down in chairs of the same height, with heads at the same level and parallel with borders and footlights; or for them all to be standing bolt-upright with bodies parallel to the proscenium arch. The way an actor stands or sits can be indicative not only of character, but of character relationship. Only a brazen charwoman being interviewed in the drawing-room, would sit back in a relaxed position in an easy chair as though she had been invited to afternoon tea. Nor would her prospective mistress adopt the same sitting position as she would in the intimacy of the family circle, even though she was in her own home. Two people, though of the same social set, sitting in exactly the same pose at either end of the settee, appear very unnatural.

Fitting the Parts into the Whole

The producer will conserve his energy by concentrating on one thing at a time. When he is rehearsing with actors, even if only watching a run through, he should keep his eyes, and his mind, on the immediate concern of interpretation. If he tries to divide his attention between the stage and administrative affairs, both will suffer. Interruption for consultations with, say, wardrobe mistress or property master during rehearsals may mean diverting the producer's attention from the stage at a crucial moment, with consequent waste of valuable time. Discussion with back-stage workers should be kept separate from acting rehearsals, as should rehearsals for lighting and stage management, until the various groups are proficient enough for integration at general rehearsals.

The appointment of a stage director can be a great boon to a producer. The stage director acts as liaison officer between the producer and the several departments and can take over rehearsals, or actual production in an emergency. The best introduction to dramatic production is through stage direction under an experienced producer though it is optimistic to expect such an office to exist in any other than the more ambitious dramatic groups.

It is assumed that the producer would not embark on a production before ensuring that key positions for administrative and working purposes were filled. In an established dramatic society some of these are held permanently by the same people but appointments are often made for each production. The number of offices depends, among other things, upon the size of the group, as does the question of combining acting with administrative or back-stage work. One group may have a dozen people to undertake the work; another only half a dozen. The following list of officers can be modified, as indicated, according to the varying conditions. Some of the designations are self-explanatory and the duties of most are referred to elsewhere in the book.

Business and Organization
1. Production Secretary
2. Business Manager (and front-of-house staff)
3. Publicity Manager

Production and Stage Team
4. Stage Director
5. Stage Manager
6. First Assistant Stage Manager
7. Second Assistant Stage Manager
8. Lighting Director
9. Assistant Lighting Director
10. Wardrobe Mistress (and assistants)
11. Property Master
12. Designer

(The Prompter is not included in the above list because, like the Producer, he works directly with the actors.)

Some of these offices may have to be 'doubled' but it is better to begin with this analysis of the work to be done, even though individual people cannot be found for the respective tasks. If we eliminate the stage manager, who will be in charge back-stage, and the lighting director who will be at the switchboard during performances unless in exceptional cases, many of the offices could be combined with acting: though this should be done only when no other course is open. It is harassing for an actor to have to think of extraneous work on the nights of the performance. In a small amateur group it might be an easy matter for one person to undertake all the business and organization, which unifies 1, 2 and 3. Where this work is too heavy, 1 and 4, 2 and 3, 4 and 12, 5 and 12, 6 and 9, 7 and 10, or 9 and 11 could be combined. The producer may also have to undertake 4 or 12 or both. If the actual requirements for a particular production are understood at the outset and no one is forced into work of which he is incapable, the allocation of duties should offer no insurmountable difficulties.

Words! Words! Words!

There are innumerable contradictions in the theatre. Though we must at all times insist on the words of the author, being faithful to the text and extracting the fullest possible meaning from it, there are some actors who say, rather impatiently, that it doesn't matter what one does or says within reason, so long as it is done or said with conviction. It is true that the actor sometimes transcends the mere iteration of words and by creating atmosphere carries his audience with him above and beyond the literal sense of the words. There have been occasions when great actors have appeared to transform the trite or the trivial into high art by sheer force of acting ability. There have been productions in which the sordid has seemed momentarily beautiful, plays in which the actor has risen above his material and criticism has been confounded. Dame Peggy Ashcroft made Hester in *The Deep Blue Sea* into something out of the Ibsen stable—which is not to denigrate a playwright of the quality of Terence Rattigan!

To go from the sublime to the ridiculous and use an illustration from personal experience:

A quarter of a century ago I was playing juveniles and character parts in a north country weekly repertory company, which presented a 'blood-and-thunder' every three months—*Sweeney Todd, the Demon Barber*. I had the experience of sandwiching *Maria Marten or The Mystery of the Red Barn*—in which I played

Carlos the Gypsy, a Bow Street runner and The Hangman—in between Browning in *The Barretts of Wimpole Street* and doubling Harry and Simon in Barrie's *Mary Rose*.

We played it 'straight' with the best stage settings I have ever seen in 'Maria'. A lorry load of real earth was delivered for the murder scene. Corder bashed Maria with the spade. She staggered screaming into the wings and was out again like a shot after the S.M. had daubed the down-stage side of her face from a jar of raspberry jam, falling back prone upstage of the clods of clay with which Corder proceeded to bury her, to the accompaniment of a rapid crescendo from the orchestra and dimming of lights.

I was rather young and a little superior for the full-blooded treatment of the production. When it came to Carlos's lines in the love scene—'Maria, before I met you, the sky was not so blue, the grass not so green, nor the forest flowers so fair,' I blanched and asked, 'Must I really say that?' The old character men and women were (rightly) indignant and said 'You must believe in it', and 'All you have to do is to be sincere'—and so forth. We worked from various tattered scripts with three or four word cues, no two of them agreeing with each other. The old-timers argued as to which was the more genuine; how one had played it with Charlie Denville and if anyone knew 'Maria' Charlie did! Whether we should include the Gypsy Encampment—the camp-fire was so colourful and the gypsy songs on which none of them could agree except that they lent such atmosphere and provided marvellous contrast, etc., etc.

But the argument which came nearest to blows was between the producer and 'William Corder'. He was a grand actor of the old school and we shall never see his like again—he still owes me five pounds! They fought about the height—or depth—of the drop in the gallows, of which the producer was inordinately proud. ('They've never seen one like this before'.) It was a truly terrifying spectacle with a sixteen-foot drop and a platform with a trap consisting of two hinged flaps on which Corder had to stand, with the only support from below a 'four-by-two' length of timber hinged in the middle. On the cue—Carlos pulling a non-practical lever such as were used in railway signal boxes at the time—the S.M. pulled a rope attached to the 'four-by-two' near the hinge; the trap collapsed and Corder disappeared, complete with noose round his neck, leaving Carlos standing precipitously on a shaking ledge twelve inches wide.

The gallows scene was to be played in mime only, behind a gauze, with appropriate orchestral accompaniment. Corder insisted that the drop was too deep. He didn't want to play it and if he did so he should be paid 'danger money'. The producer claimed that there had never been anything more serious than a broken leg in 'Maria' but eventually reduced the gallows drop by a couple of feet. Then Corder found another grievance. He thought the mime was a good idea—but oh dear! this modern stuff!—so long as he could have a last word before fate caught up with him. After all, Corder was the lead, the audience would expect it and he'd always done a swan-song for 'Charlie'. The tussle for supremacy continued throughout the week and at last the producer relented, *after* the dress rehearsal, and the fatal speech wasn't rehearsed. 'Do what the hell you like and may you break your neck' was *his* final word as he stalked out of the theatre. I tracked down the S.M. to tell him he would have a word-cue as well as an action-cue for the 'drop'. Corder told us the cue; 'You who witness the fate of William Corder/Have more respect for law and order.'

At the performance Corder was worried, as indeed I was, because it hadn't been rehearsed. Nevertheless, all was going swimmingly and we came to the gallows-scene which met with a round of applause when the curtain came up on it. Enter Corder in white shirt-blouse followed by Carlos disguised in flowing cloak and mask . . . Corder up the steps to the gallows, then Carlos, in slow march to the ominous, muted 'Ta-rah-dah-dah-BOOM-dah' of the orchestra. Corder on to the trap gingerly, Carlos balancing on his narrow ledge. The drums fade out. I place the noose round his neck, feeling surreptitiously to make sure that the rope is free to slide through the cable-wheel. Then my hand on the lever for his cue . . . the sweat pouring down his face . . . he took a deep breath, looked up to the gods and bawled, 'All you who witness the fate of William Corder . . .' pause . . . out of the corner of my eye I saw the look of terror which goes with the 'dry-up' . . . I turned in on him and 'mouthed' 'law and order' and like the trouper he was, he gave a withering glance to the back row of the pit and bellowed—

'Er . . . something . . . something . . . HARRY LAUDER!'
At least it rhymed. Down into the depths he went, with me almost after him from shock . . . drums up to full . . . Blackout! Followed by loud and prolonged—no! not laughter!—*Applause.*

The point of the story is that when we went, shamefacedly, into the bar after the show, we discovered that the audience was so excited that not one of them had noticed the gaffe. Neither, incidentally had the S.M. This was no miracle, just a bit of theatre. It could not have happened at the beginning, before the audience was warmed up. We had them with us by that time.

It has been claimed that *Hamlet* has the best beginning of any play in the English language. Yet this wonderful opportunity is sometimes missed in amateur productions. Here is the script:

FIRST ACT
Scene One

Elsinore. A platform before the castle.
Francisco at his post. Enter to him Bernardo.
Bernardo: Who's there?
Francisco: Nay, answer me: stand, and unfold yourself.

The atmosphere which pervades the whole play is implicit in the first speech of two words. Bernardo, who has come to *relieve* the guard is so much under the influence of fear and agitation that he, a trained soldier, forgets himself so far as to give the challenge as though *he* were *on* guard and says, 'Who's there?' This reversal of the natural order of things is a shock to Francisco whose imagination is probably already filled with the dread of the unnatural. He has been alone in the cold and dark for some hours and he replies 'Nay, (*you*) answer *me: stand* and unfold *yourself*.' If Bernardo's challenge is given as though conditions were perfectly normal and Francisco's reply is made without even surprise as 'Nay, *answer* me: stand, and *unfold* yourself', the whole point is lost. Shakespeare was too good a dramatist to keep his audience waiting until the end of Act One, Scene 4, for the bald statement of Marcellus, 'Something is rotten in the state of Denmark.' This is only one example of interpretation being ruined by the producer's failure to see the value of simple emphasis—hitting the right word to produce the exact meaning.

Amateur producers are not the only offenders in this respect. In a professional production of *Julius Caesar* there were half a dozen examples of this kind. Two of these will suffice for illustration. In the first scene a crowd of plebeians are making holiday to celebrate Caesar's victorious return to Rome. Enter Marullus,

a Tribune of the old régime, loyal to Pompey, Caesar's pre-
decessor, who cries angrily:

> 'Wherefore rejoice? What conquest brings he home?
> What tributaries follow him to Rome
> To grace in captive bonds his chariot wheels?
> You blocks, you stones, you worse than senseless things.'

(Obviously, one would think, 'you *worse* than blocks and stones.')
   But the actor said 'You worse than *senseless* things', setting
up an antithesis between 'blocks and stones' and 'senseless
things' and thereby suggesting that blocks and stones have
sense! Later, in the Forum scene, Antony says:

> 'I am no orator as Brutus is . . .
>   . . . but were I Brutus
> And Brutus Antony, there were an Antony
> Would ruffle up your spirits, and put a tongue
> In every wound of Caesar, that would move
> The stones of Rome to rise and mutiny.'

(Move, not only the people of Rome, but the *stones* of Rome.)
   The actor said 'that would move the stones of *Rome* to rise . . .'
so that one member of the audience asked himself—but aren't
we *in* Rome, and if not, where?
   Words and phrases have dramatic value only in relation to the
context. Occasionally there are several possible meanings but a
producer who allowed the opposite of the meaning where there
is no alternative as in the three examples given could not be
expected to exercise discrimination when necessary.
   Who is to decide on the emphasis in Lady Macbeth's reply to
Macbeth's query, 'If we should fail?' in the scene before the
murder (Act One, Scene 7). She replies:

> 'We fail.
> But screw your courage to the sticking-place,
> And we'll not fail: . . .'

Some editors use a question mark; 'We fail?' but punctuation
is a matter of opinion in Shakespeare. It could equally well be a
statement; 'We fail!' or even simply 'We fail.' Is it '*We* fail?' or

'We *fail*!' The choice would affect 'And we'll not fail!' If we decide on '*We* fail?' we might decide to hit the other word when we come to 'And we'll not *fail*:' Or we could say, 'We *fail*: . . . And we'll *not* fail.' Or we could give equal stress to both words in each case, '*We fail* . . . *Not fail*.' Or what about '*We* (pause) fail?' . . . 'And we'll *not* (pause) *fail*!'?

> Does Hamlet say: 'To *be* or *not* to be'?
> 'To *be* or not to *be*'?
> or
> 'To *be* (pause) or *not* (pause) to *be*'?

In the opening speech of Act One, Scene 5, Lady Macbeth, referring to her husband says:

> '. . . yet do I fear thy nature,
> It is too full o' the milk of human kindness
> To catch the nearest way . . .'

Does she mean that he is too sentimental, that he 'is too full of the milk of human *kindness*' or that he is too human (being herself monstrous), that he 'is too full of the milk of *human*-kindness'? Authoritative opinion favours the second interpretation. The classic howler in *Macbeth* is in the speech immediately after the murder (Act Two, Scene 2) when Macbeth says:

> 'Will all great Neptune's ocean wash this blood
> Clean from my hand? No; this my hand will rather
> The multitudinous seas incarnadine,
> Making the green one red.'

No one who had observed question and answer and noted that 'all great Neptune's ocean' and 'the multitudinous seas' and 'the green' were different descriptions of the same thing, could make the mistake of saying 'making the *green* one, *red*', i.e. making the green one into a red one. The word 'one' relates to 'red', not 'green', and requires a pause between 'green' and 'one red'; 'making ('all great Neptune's ocean' or 'the multitudinous seas' or 'the green') *one* red' (i.e. entirely red).

Certain pronunciations which are not current are occasionally used for the sake of the verse in Shakespeare, e.g.

'My manors, rents, revenues I forgo' (reVENues)
(*Richard the Second*. Act Four, Scene I, Line 212)

and some purists would even insist on

'As in a vault, an ancient receptacle! (receptAHcle)
(*Romeo and Juliet*. Act Four, Scene 3, line 39)

In no less a place than Stratford, the actor playing Edgar was heard to say:

'The lamentable change is from the best'
(*King Lear*, Act Four, Scene 1, line 5)

'*Lam*entable' is an example of 'Recessive Accent', where the accent is on the first syllable, as in, '*form*idable', '*comm*endable', '*des*picable', '*con*troversy'. (For further reference see Fowler's *Modern English Usage*.) The actor or producer may justifiably claim that he was using the older pronunciation; even so, it flagrantly upsets the rhythm of the blank verse. In ordinary conversation alternative pronunciations are permissible but for stage purposes authority should be the guide, especially in verse plays. The producer should always have a pronouncing dictionary near for ready reference; a reliable standard work is Daniel Jones's *An English Pronouncing Dictionary*.

Interpretation

THERE are as many interpretations of any part as there are actors who have played the part. A play is made up of *people*; their actions, reactions and interactions, whether they are figments of the imagination or dramatizations of historical characters. How does the producer decide what sort of people?

To begin with he has the speeches—the dialogue which reflects the behaviour and attitudes of the characters, which have to be interpreted through the medium of the actors. These actors are different people from the characters in the play; they have their own individual personalities and may not be in sympathy with the characters they are asked to interpret. The actor's approach to any part is almost purely subjective and we should not take too seriously the charges of selfishness so frequently levelled against actors. For an actor to be objective or academic in his study of the character could deprive it of the qualities necessary to bring it to life on the stage. The producer has to try to be objective and dispassionate about *individual* characters in order to see the relationship of one to another. Subjectivity and objectivity are probably the qualities which differentiate actor and producer more than any others. Someone has said that there is a god-like quality about the ideal producer, who wills his subjects, the actors, into bending to his wishes. He can, if he so desires, use the actors to give an entirely opposite interpretation from that which the author intended.

Macklin, in the eighteenth century, when the leading actor was the producer, transformed the character of Shylock from that of low comedian popular for some time previously, to one of tragic hero and inspired Pope to write:

> *This is the Jew*
> *That Shakespeare drew.*

Sir Laurence Olivier, under the direction of Peter Brook at Stratford, made something previously undreamed of from Titus Andronicus. The plays of Tchekhov were treated in the tragic manner when first produced in this country, until it was realized that they were originally intended as comedies by the author who had objected to Stanislavski's interpretation in Tcheckhov's own lifetime.

If professional producers can read such a variety of interpretations into a play, it must be doubly difficult for the amateur to decide on the author's intention. The author often attends rehearsals with a professional producer, for consultation and elucidation of ambiguities. The amateur can only use his own good sense; the best he can do is to read and re-read the play, giving due regard to all the possible alternatives and by a process of elimination decide on the interpretation which most nearly approaches truth as he sees it. Having embarked on production, if, when the play begins to take shape, he becomes aware of anything false, which had eluded him in the reading he will be wise to admit his mistake without hesitation. He must take his courage in both hands and make the necessary alterations regardless of criticism from the cast or anyone else.

The temperament of the actor may be as different from the producer's as it is from that of the character. Can the actor say what the author wants the character to say in the way the producer wants it said? Does it sound convincing when the actor tries to imitate the producer's interpretation? Or is the producer more convinced of the seeming truth, though it differs from his original idea, in the way the actor says it? What will be the effect on the audience of each of the two ways? How does it relate to the context? Does it alter radically the producer's idea of the author's intention? There are more ways than one of speaking the same truth.

The producer is on an adventure of discovery. If he is compassionate he will not hate even Iago, despicable as his behaviour appears. He must find out why a character behaves in a particular manner—what makes him 'tick'. One can admire the cleverness of a producer who is capable of forcing characters in a play into a particular mould to prove a pet theory but one might doubt his integrity.

The reputation of Berthold Brecht as a playwright is established beyond doubt and his theory of 'alienation' is exciting to anyone interested in the theatre. The theory was examined by Herbert Luthy in an article in *Encounter* (July, 1956) an extract from which is given below, followed by another extract from an article by Henry Adler in *Twentieth Century* (August, 1956) describing a proposal of Brecht's to present *Hamlet* in a *new* way, which was an inversion of hitherto accepted values:

(1) 'He (Brecht) may go down in theatrical history rather as a great director than as a great dramatist . . . The truth is that Brecht for many years has not been a playwright but a *régisseur*. The theory of "epic" theatre itself is intended for the director, not the dramatic author. According to this theory, the action that takes place on the stage is not the content of the drama but the object of a demonstration intended for the critical eye of the audience, to be taken apart and analysed sociologically. Since Brecht transformed himself from a poet into a "teacher", his aim has been, not to create dramas but to dissect them— and for that purpose other men's dramas serve as well as his own.

In the East German edition of his works published some months ago, he has once again made "ideological improvements", so that now there exists simultaneously, for *every one* of his plays, and even his prefaces, an authorized version for East Germany and another, equally authorized version for West Germany.'

At one time Brecht had a scheme for rewriting *Hamlet* from the viewpoint of historical materialism . . . for which he has offered a sample in the form of a long "Interlude for Hamlet" . . . in which it is made clear that Hamlet's hesitation corresponds to "the new bourgeois point of view", in which commerce and well-being—the Danish fish trade—rank higher than honour, while Hamlet's decision to act represents a relapse into "the feudal point of view".'

(2) 'In an attempt to estrange sentimental attraction and leave the way clear for moral judgement, Brecht plans to cast Hamlet as a short fat man (like Burbage) so that he may be recognized as a wastrel. It is argued that Hamlet's father was an inefficient ruler who deserved liquidation, and that Claudius, who proves himself an able administrator, is the most admirable character in the play.'

Brecht died before these plans materialized and just before his company, 'Berliner Ensemble', made its first visit to London, where they met with tremendous approbation.

While it is not intended to draw a parallel between the theories of Brecht and his predecessors the intellectual approach of the actor and audience is by no means revolutionary. We are told authoritatively that, in the eighteenth century, 'Diderot's theory is to regard the character objectively, without personally feeling any of the emotions portrayed,' and in the nineteenth century, 'Coquelin (Aîné) is accepted as the most successful exponent of this method.' And what of Bernard Shaw in the early twentieth century? Apart from *St. Joan* and to a much lesser extent *Candida*, his appeal is one of reason rather than feeling. Both the offering of the actor and the reception of the audience are on the intellectual plane, not the emotional. Even Brecht's socializing of *Hamlet* had been anticipated in 1932, by the Russian producer Akimov at the Vakhtangov Theatre.[1]

Imitation in the theatre results in staleness; freshness of interpretation is vital for healthy theatre, but innovation of interpretation for its own sake or for the purpose of propaganda is a perversion of an artistic medium. Unless the original creation —the play—was intended to reveal social injustice or stupidity, the producer misuses his power by making it appear to do so.

On the other hand, the belief that modern audiences can be made to think as Elizabethans, by attempts to recreate the conditions of the theatre and even the speech of the times, shows a disregard for elementary psychology. Theatre research is a laudable study but its place is the academy rather than the theatre. Experimental theatre is the life-blood of dramatic enterprise but insistence on discarding established principles for new techniques does not necessarily mean progress.

The arena theatre and theatre-in-the-round, are little more than extensions of Elizabethan theatre with its projecting platform and the audience on three sides. The claims made for 'improvisation' of dialogue in John Cassavetes' prize film, *Shadows*, reminds us that improvisation is as old as the *all' improviso* of the *commedia dell' arte* of sixteenth-century Italy. Method and medium are important only in so far as they reflect truth and sincerity of purpose. The brilliance of the direction of the B.B.C. series *The Age of Kings*, proved that Shakespeare can be adapted for any age in any medium and still be faithful to the text. Any one of the series was as much at home on television as a fragment such as Alun Owen's *Lena! O My Lena*, which may become a television classic but which it is difficult to imagine in any other medium in the same form.

[1] Theatre in Soviet Russia, André van Gysegham.

CHAPTER FOUR

Choosing the play

No matter how experienced the amateur producer, his choice of play is limited by the technical ability of his actors. He would be foolhardy indeed who chose a Restoration comedy for a group of beginners. The extremes of dramatic possibilities, highly stylized period material and the apparent spontaneity of Theatre Workshop kind are only for experienced amateur actors. This does not exclude some of the finest drama in the language, including Shakespeare and Shaw. There are innumerable 'actor-proof' plays, whose language alone will 'carry' inexperienced actors. Even so, only the best of Shakespeare and Shaw are recommended. The emotional content of some of the Shakespearean tragedies compensates very often for lack of technique in the actors whereas many of the comedies fall flat without a modicum of technical ability. Although it has been said earlier that Shaw is intellectual theatre the plays are saved from the purely didactic by his brilliant wit and superb craftsmanship. His language 'rolls off the tongue'—with intelligent production and sufficient rehearsal—as does that of very few playwrights. If the actor has a sound pair of lungs, a resonant voice, good enunciation and rapid articulation, plus a mind capable of appreciating what Shaw has to say, he might 'get away with it'. Some of Barrie and most of Galsworthy are fairly safe for trying out fresh people. Although it is doubtful whether the whimsy of the first or the moralizing of the second would meet with the sympathy of young people of today, their plays are mostly well-made. Ibsen's plays with the larger casts and more even distribution of lines are excellent in later translations. Each one tells a story and the dramatic construction is nearly perfect. It is hardly necessary to say that parts such as Hedda Gabler, or Rebecca West in *Rosmersholm*, or Solness in *The Master Builder* are not recommended for beginners but a play such as *Pillars of Society* could be *got through* effectively even if it wasn't *played*.

In the average amateur dramatic production one has to be prepared to sacrifice at least some of the substance for the shadow by comparison with a professional production. The producer looks for the play which retains the greatest amount of substance in production. A first-class play within the limits suggested will almost carry itself providing there is no single part too long and too difficult for an inexperienced actor to sustain, although Sybil Thorndike is reputed as having once said that there could be no such thing as a bad performance of *Hamlet*.

The producer must beware of first impressions; of a play which leaps from the page on reading or romps home in professional production. No one of experience would jump to the conclusion that all that was necessary for a Joan Littlewood production, or *Lock up Your Daughters* with which The Mermaid opened, was vitality and high spirits. Some productions may appear to be nothing more than highly developed professional charades but the operative words are 'highly professional'. They usually combine several theatrical conventions requiring various techniques. It is rare to find a cast of amateurs who can act, sing and dance equally well.

The audience must also be taken into consideration when choice of a play is made. There is more to it than the question of sophistication. They may be prepared to accept and enjoy to the full a play in the West End theatre which they might not accept if played by friends or acquaintances in the village hall at home, where they don't enjoy the same degree of anonymity in the auditorium.

The producer has to decide how far he can stretch his audience's 'willing suspension of disbelief' where actors and audience are part of the same community. Mary Smith might be more acceptable to her friends as the wife of a country doctor than as a blue-blooded duchess and Mrs Jones might try to cover her embarrassment when she meets her in the butcher's the morning after the night before when Mary was a prostitute; but she may not come to the next show! It all depends on how closed your dramatic community is, but even in large towns there is a degree of intimacy between players and audience which does not exist in the West End of London.

Between the wars authors of the Frederick Lonsdale and Noël Coward school wrote plays about lords and ladies in their manor houses, or public school types in their suburban villas being slightly naughty for the benefit of middle-class audiences as a change from Sunday church parade. Since the war there has been a social inversion of the characters and settings in a certain type of play in which there is probably greater verisimilitude but an equally limited range, from products of 'red-brick' universities educated beyond their intelligence to pregnant teenagers, prostitutes, pimps and perverts. Both types of play deal with minorities —the extreme ends of the social scale. Each social group has always existed and in each case is given a prominence out of proportion to its social significance. Both are represented with more balance in Shakespeare—who knew where to put his fops, and his bawds! Ibsen's plays are given middle-class settings but they deal with universal truths.

No producer worth his salt would allow himself to be browbeaten on to the 'bandwaggon' of modernity. There can be nothing more dreary than a topical play even a few months old. Nor should he be persuaded that a play is 'dated' because it is momentarily out of fashion. All the best plays are 'dated'— including everything worth while from *Everyman* to *Juno and the Paycock*. They have stood the test of time. The rest are museum pieces known only to lecturers on dramatic literature in universities. Who wants to produce *Ralph Roister Doister* even if it was the first English comedy? Here is a conversation between a producer and a member of his company: Guess which is the producer!

'Why can't we do a comedy?'

'What kind of comedy?'

'Well—you know—something funny.'

'Good, we've got centuries of them to choose from.'

'Oh, but we must do something modern.'

'Yes, but what do you mean by modern?'

'Well—you know—not in costume.'

'Ah! now we're getting somewhere.'

'Of course, I don't mean farce, you've already told us that it requires experience and a special technique.'

'Good, it's a great help to limit the field. Mention some titles.'

'Well, I was given a good one to read last week. A nice story it had, with a simple domestic background . . . *Bird in Hand*.'

'Ye-es. Of course it *is* costume of a kind, and—er—don't you think it's a little dated?'

'All right, you mention one. Something different, say a farcical comedy.'

'No, I'd rather the suggestions came from the group at this stage.'

'Oh, go on!'

(with both feet) '*Charley's Aunt.*'

(gasps) 'But that's older than *Bird in Hand.*'

'I'm sorry. Did I mention age?'

'Yes! *Charley's Aunt* is more dated than *Bird in Hand* isn't it?'

'They are both dated. But one is dated and evergreen and the other is dated and mouldy' (at which he bit out his tongue).

Incidentally, *Charley's Aunt* is not seriously suggested for amateur production, except with a highly experienced cast. It is an example of a classic piece—in a theatrical, not a literary sense.

How 'modern' is a modern play? A good play is new to each generation. Take for example the first play of Arnold Wesker's trilogy, *Chicken Soup with Barley.* This was a great draw—the very latest thing—at the Royal Court Theatre. It was a thrill to see so many 'pony-tails' and 'jeans' in the live theatre. It was enjoyed by the young because it was 'new' and by the old because it was good old-fashioned domestic drama! After Shelagh Delaney's and Brendan Behan's mixtures of everything from music-hall to melodrama in a single production, here we were treated to the novelty of a well-made play, moving and dramatic, with curtains coming down on a climax; a story with a beginning, a middle and an end; and without one song or dance! Wesker daring to be simple as well as sincere—a man with singleness of mind: the O'Casey of the East End—with apologies to *The Plough and the Stars.*

The amateur producer who tried to emulate, or even imitate, Joan Littlewood's Theatre Workshop productions would be courageous indeed but in Wesker there is strong characterization and a burning passion, qualities which might see a young amateur cast without technique through a production, playing it 'from the heart'. There are contemporary plays of ideas ranging from 'off-beat' to conformity, to catch the imagination of the young. Worthy of consideration for reading at least are the four Johns —Osborne, Arden, Whiting and Mortimer. It is a long time since a theatre quinquennium has provided such variety as *Look Back in Anger, Serjeant Musgrave's Dance, The Devils* and *The Wrong Side of the Park.* While no amateur actress could be expected to give as striking a performance in the last-named as Margaret Leighton's, a good amateur production could be more satisfying than the television presentation, not because of the failure of Brenda Bruce and the cast but for the reason that a true interpretation is only possible in the theatre. Television changed a good play into a documentary of a psychiatric case-history.

It has been suggested, with reservations, that costume plays are easier than contemporary plays for beginners. One of the worst mistakes is to choose plays about actors and actresses, especially in theatrical settings. The average amateur is handicapped enough without trying to create the illusion of larger than larger-than-life people in artificial surroundings, very often on an improvised stage! Plays of this kind are usually comedies, which does not ease the technical difficulties. Consider the sets alone for, e.g. Anouilh's *Colombe* or J. B. Priestley's *The Good Companions*. The real audience is supposed to be looking through the back of the stage and on to the imaginary audience through the stage-within-the-stage. The leading actress in *Colombe* is expected to emulate Sarah Bernhardt—or at least think she does! Remember it was the quality of Sir Laurence Olivier's acting which was responsible for the success of *The Entertainer*, not the script. Even a short play like Terence Rattigan's *Harlequinade* is a representation of rather *passé* actors one of whom has to say 'I've never been a good actor'. An actor has to be very good indeed to act a bad actor. Plays about the theatre seem to have a fascination for amateurs. Both Rattigan and Coward are professional and prolific writers, each of them providing material eminently suitable for amateur production and it is surprising to find amateur societies choosing, for instance, *Hay Fever* or *Waiting in the Wings* from a repertoire as vast as Coward's. The only point in favour of *Hay Fever* is that it is at least set in the country, but it requires an exceptional amateur comedy actress for Judith Bliss. Lennox Robinson's *Drama at Innish* which is about a touring company in Ireland is easier, if only because the theatre in Ireland has never been as professionalized, nor the actors as far removed from ordinary people as they are in England.

Very often the producer has to take into account the educational and social background of a young cast, as well as their capacity for intellectual appreciation and their technical ability. He can fall into grievous error here. Adjudicators are sometimes bewildered by a producer's defence against criticism of the choice of a play which could not have been saved by a combination of Gielgud, Edith Evans, Olivier and Guthrie. When suggestions have been made of plays which the cast could at least have attempted the producer has replied, 'But my cast couldn't touch that. It's much too difficult,' on the principle that the poorer the actors the worse must be the play! It is difficult to follow the logic of the argument that bad acting must be matched by puerile dialogue and impossible situations. Plays—for want of a better word—are sometimes chosen for youth clubs, for instance, on which no self-respecting teacher would waste the time for one lesson with a class of educationally subnormal children. Even a poor performance of a good play leaves the actors, and the audience, with a modicum of substance. Chesterton once said that a thing worth doing was worth doing badly. T. S. Eliot is more specific, especially if for the word 'auditor' we read 'actor' in the following paragraph:

'In a play of Shakespeare you get several levels of significance. For the simplest auditors there is the plot, for the more thoughtful the characters and conflict of characters, for the more literary the words and phrasing, for the more musically sensitive the rhythm, and for auditors of greater sensitiveness and understanding a meaning which reveals itself gradually. At none of these levels is the auditor bothered by the presence of that which he does not understand or by the presence of that in which he is not interested.' (*Selected Prose*.)

The producer has to do the best he can with his available resources. He is not dependent on his cast for quality of play. Eliot gives him the procedure which he follows as far as he can.

Take *Hamlet* again for an example. The bare bones of the plot is little more than a crime detection story with Hamlet as the sleuth and Claudius as the suspected murderer. Characterization has never been a strong feature of the 'who-done-it' and so we add Eliot's second level of significance to plot. If we cannot go on to Eliot's next level for the *more literary*, we are not doing badly even if we are limited to plot, character and conflict of character in a play of quality. We can still have a tolerable production—at that level.

Some youth club producers avoid suggesting titles which might bear the stigma of dramatic literature for fear of being dubbed 'eggheads'. If the purpose of drama in clubs is no higher than keeping young people off the streets the choice of one-act plays which are churned out by the hundred for an easy market suggests that the cure is worse than the disease. Good one-act plays are few and far between but the tried-and-true ones are always new to young people and if they are compared with third-rate trash they will be given preference nine times out of ten. There are too many for individual mention but Tchekhov's *The Bear* and *The Proposal* nearly always meet with a ready response from teen-agers. The poetically minded might try Yeats, Fry or Synge and the more venturesome, Ionesco.

Selections from full-length plays are preferable to many one-act plays, are more complete even out of context and are more satisfactory in plot and character. Again only one example can be given, from Pirandello's *Right You Are—If You Think You Are!* The play as a whole has philosophical and psychological significance which it is not always easy to follow, but part of the play can be taken at Eliot's first level of significance. This is the second half of the first act where most of the cast, five women and four men, are brought on the stage. The two main parts are those of Signor Ponza and Signora Frola. The excerpt begins at Signora Frola's first entrance. These two are newcomers to a small country town in Italy where Signor Ponza has recently been appointed to a civic position. Some of the civic chiefs, their wives and families, have been discussing the apparent mystery and peculiar domestic behaviour of Signor Ponza, his wife (who does not appear in this scene) and Signora Frola.

Signora Frola lives separately from Ponza and his wife—her supposed daughter. By subtle inference and without direct accusation we learn from her that Ponza is cruelly keeping his wife and her mother apart; that he is so much in love with his wife that he can't bear to share her with anyone else. She elicits the sympathy of her listeners and arouses their indignation and anger at Ponza's treatment of her. After her departure Ponza arrives and has a totally different story to tell. He claims that his wife is not Signora Frola's daughter. His first wife was her daughter but she was killed in an earthquake in which, he says, all his and Signora Frola's relatives were lost. He and his wife have lived through four years of persecution from Signora Frola and he is driven to confiding to the company that she, Signora Frola, is insane. Her insanity takes the form of refusing to believe that her daughter is dead and insistence in believing that Ponza's second wife is his first wife—her daughter. Ponza goes and after a short discussion by the others, Signora Frola comes in again. She guesses what he has told them and she in turn confides to them that it is Ponza who is insane. She explains that her daughter had an illness which caused the temporary separation of husband and wife. This drove him mad and he believed that she was dead. He had to be sent to a sanatorium. When he was released he held on to the obsession and refused to believe that his wife was still alive even when they met. Eventually however, he went through a second marriage ceremony with his first wife believing her to be his second. Since then both mother and daughter have humoured his whim. After Signora Frola's departure, one of the characters says 'So you want the truth, eh? The truth! the truth! Ha! Ha! Ha! Ha!' and the curtain comes down.

Who is mad and which is right?—*Right You Are—If You Think You Are!* Here is a problem, unsolved; but offering greater satisfaction than the contrived solutions of so many one-act thrillers.

Plays are written for professional production, and the legitimate theatre is a predominantly masculine profession in spite of the attraction it has for young women. One wonders what happens to the hundreds of them who aspire to the stage through the drama schools each year. In the amateur theatre also, women outnumber men to an enormous extent. Where can amateurs find good plays with a preponderance of women in the cast? The answer is for once, simple—they can't! This is an insurmountable problem in the amateur theatre. Quality of play is in inverse proportion to the number of women in the cast. There is never any difficulty in finding plays of merit for male casts but plays of equal standard for women only are very rare indeed. One can, without reference, name plays without women running concurrently at almost any time; *The Caretaker*, *Ross*, *The Long and the Short and the Tall*; one has to search over a quarter of a century for tolerable plays without any men: *Children in Uniform*, *The House of Bernarda Alba*, *The Women*.

There is more even distribution of men and women characters in the popular drawing-room play of the West End but most of these owe their success to professional personality actors and the provincialism of the audiences who support them. Attempts at

reproduction by amateurs do little more than reveal the hollowness of such plays.

There is evidence that the taste of audiences is changing for
the better, at least in the legitimate theatre. It behoves amateurs,
no matter how remote they are from London, to anticipate
greater discrimination in their own audiences. The development
of critical faculty on the part of audiences was considered of
sufficient importance for the *Daily Telegraph* to devote a leading
article to it recently.

CHAPTER FIVE

Breath control : voice production : speech training

EVERY trade has its tools, every craft its specialized knowledge, every art its technique. Most amateur actors are 'Do it Yourself' men; they are their own tool-boxes. They must know themselves. But self-knowledge is useless without application. An actor has to develop and improve his senses and faculties, the most important of which are his voice and speech. We have to be content with whatever voice nature has given us but we can improve its quality and increase its range. Cultivation of voice can be combined with exercises for effective speaking. Technically, the actor should think of speech as the end product. The retort that any normal person can speak can be met with the rejoinder that almost anyone can act, sing or dance. It is all a matter of degree in performance. Anyone can mutter, mumble and grunt, just as anyone can grimace, leap from one note to another or throw his arms and legs about. When we think of speaking, acting, singing or dancing on the stage, there is an accepted standard below which the amateur cannot afford to fall.

It is to the actor's advantage to know the physical aspects of voice before going on to the aesthetics of speech. The raw material of voice is breath. Before we can have control for flexibility and modulation in speech we must have control of breathing for voice. It is as well to define even the simplest terms and we can distinguish between voice and speech by reference to *The Encyclopaedia Britannica*:

> '*Voice* is the sound produced by the vibrations of the vocal cords, two ligaments or bands of fibrous elastic tissue situated in the larynx. Voice is to be distinguished from *speech*, which is the production of articulate sounds intended to express ideas. Many of the lower animals have voice, but none has the power of speech in the way man possesses that faculty. There may be speech without voice, as in whispering, whilst in singing a scale of musical tones, we have voice without speech.'

It is of no practical benefit to study the anatomy of the organs of voice and speech over which we have no control.

The larynx is the organ of voice, over which we can exercise only an indirect control. We can, however, not only control but develop the breathing mechanism situated below the larynx, for the improvement of voice, as we can the organs of articulation situated above the larynx for the cultivation of clearer speech.

Reference to the larynx can be dismissed in a few words. We know that the range of the human voice is about three octaves. One of the reasons for exercises in voice production is to increase the limited range of the average voice for greater flexibility. The more tense the vocal cords the higher pitch of the voice and the greater the length of the cords the lower the pitch. The intensity or loudness of voice depends on the amplitude of the movement of the vocal cords. Pitch depends on the number of vibrations per second. The ratio of the length of the adult male vocal cords to those of the female is three to two and generally men's voices are lower pitched and stronger than those of women.

AUDIBILITY is the first requirement of the actor and depends on the control of the breath stream. An elementary knowledge of the breathing mechanism is a help to this end. To begin with we might compare the difference between tranquil breathing and breathing for voice. Ordinarily, we breathe to keep ourselves alive; we inhale to supply oxygen to the blood-stream and exhale to remove carbon dioxide from it. Breath is taken at regular intervals and in equal amounts with a sub-conscious action. Frequency of respiration is affected by muscular exertion, age, temperature and condition of health.

In VOICE PRODUCTION, breathing is irregular and the quantity of breath is determined by the length of phrase or volume of voice required.

The torso can be compared with a double-storeyed building, with the *abdomen* on the ground floor and the *thorax* on the upper. The two are separated by the *diaphragm*, a large, single group of muscles forming the floor of the chest and the roof of the abdomen. In tranquil breathing, during inhalation, there is a slight expansion of the lower chest at the front and sides, with some protrusion of the abdomen, all of which is an involuntary action.

Breathing for voice production exercises is a voluntary action. Expansion of the ribs and diaphragm alone is cultivated with protrusion of the abdominal muscles reduced to a minimum. The result is more direct control of the breath stream on the vocal cords. Imagine the lung as a wind instrument in the centre of which is a column of air about ten inches long being directed on a pair of reeds—the vocal cords.

INTERCOSTAL DIAPHRAGMATIC breathing is the method advocated for sustained speech or song. The intercostal muscles control the action of the ribs. For inhalation they expand drawing the ribs upwards and outwards. At the same time the diaphragm is lowered to a position convex to the abdomen. Thus the breath cavity is formed supported from below by a firm abdominal wall.

Whereas chest *expansion* is practised by the 'You too can have a body like mine' school of physical culturists for muscular development, the actor practises chest *contraction* for breath control to produce voice. Needless to say, there can be no contraction without expansion but the actor or speaker has to decide the best means to his particular end. Any exercises which induce muscular rigidity are harmful to the voice. Herein lies the difference between voice production and voice destruction. For instance, *full* breathing for the sole purpose of chest expansion, for muscular development, results in loss of control during exhalation because of over-tensed muscles. *Deep* breathing allows for alternating states of relaxation and tension without which there can be no control of breath or voice. Intercostal-diaphragmatic exercises should be practised, first for breathing alone and later allied with vocal exercises.

Faulty methods of breathing for production of voice can easily be checked, for example, *abdominal* breathing, which can be described as voice production by remote control. This means that there is no support from below for the intercostal-diaphragmatic muscles. The abdominal muscles are distended instead of forming a firm base for the lower chest mechanism, which is allowed to sag. Consequently more muscular effort from a greater distance is required for direction of the column of air to the vocal cords. This method of breathing can be exhausting if practised while speaking for any length of time. The bad effect on the voice could be appreciated in a long part requiring considerable vocal effort. Another incorrect method of breathing for voice is known as *clavicular breathing*, perhaps commoner among women than men. The lower chest mechanism is hardly used at all. An attempt is made to draw air into the upper regions of the lungs by raising the shoulders, which results in congestion of air immediately below the larynx. The breath cannot be *directed* to the vocal cords. It simply escapes through them with considerable loss of the vibration essential in the initial stages of voice production.

Sore throat and undue fatigue are the commonest manifestations of bad voice production. No actor should suffer from throat trouble as a direct result of using the voice. Anyone who starts off, as it were, in top gear at the rise of the curtain, is too intense and holds nothing in reserve, will make a nervous wreck, not only of himself but of his fellow actors, and probably of the audience. A strident voice or staccato delivery can be the cause of nervous excitement both on the stage and in the auditorium. It is the quiet, clear voice which induces a general atmosphere of confidence and repose and should always be attempted except where the dramatic situation demands otherwise. Inexperienced actors sometimes confuse the use of the staccato voice with 'keeping up the pitch', in comedy for instance. How often do we hear the producer calling in despair, 'Don't force it—let it come!'?

It is in the actor's own interest and in the interest of the production to avoid nervous tensions which are revealed through the voice. He should adopt as relaxed an attitude as the part allows right from the beginning. We must distinguish between the dramatic tension of the play and the muscular tensions of voice and speech as a result of nervousness or lack of control. One or two examples of the latter will suffice for illustration.

Constriction of the muscles which control the action of the larynx, which is often accompanied by a slight 'catch' in the throat or hesitation during speech. Some nervous speakers try to overcome this by stretching the neck and shooting the chin up and out. Such action does not relieve the condition—on the contrary, it aggravates it. Consider the effect on the tone and pitch of the voice. Try it and you will find that the skin over the larynx tightens. Consequently the delicate muscles which control the action of the larynx are also tightened. But if the neck is kept in a relaxed position with the chin held reasonably down there is a considerable improvement in the resonating quality of the voice. Hold one finger, very lightly, on the protruding part of the hyoid bone (or Adam's apple). Take two notes, the lowest and highest of an octave, and sing them on a vowel sound, repeating alternately. You should feel an up and down movement of the cartilage corresponding to the height or depth of the note. This simple exercise demonstrates that the more relaxed the muscles the greater the control of pitch and tone of voice.

Tightness of the jaw is another indication of nervousness. Muscular rigidity causes the lower jaw to become almost fixed. Hypertension at the joint results in the speaker forcing his voice through clenched teeth, reducing the resonating cavity of the mouth. Anyone with this tendency should practise dropping the lower jaw for flexibility and muscular relaxation. We all do this instinctively on occasion; we yawn for relief from the tension of boredom.

Further evidence of nervousness is to be found in *tightness of the chest* and *breathlessness*. The causes are constriction of the intercostal muscles between the ribs and spasms of the diaphragm. When speech is attempted the breath is taken in short gasps, and as there is no direct muscular control, there is an instinctive closure of the glottis to retain the air. During exhalation there is no muscular direction of air so that when the vocal cords are parted for the action of speech, the breath escapes, or is only partly vocalized, resulting in 'breathy tone'.

There are many and varied factors contributing to incorrect use of the voice and the way to eradicate faults in voice production is to see to first things first. Even an actor with a good voice will be well advised to preserve it by conservation of energy, providing the maximum of effort with the minimum of strain, or the best quality of voice with economy of breath. Good health is a pre-requisite for good voice and correct breathing is a sound basis for both. Begin with a simple exercise for testing inter-costal-diaphragmatic control:

Stand—or sit well back in the angle of a hard chair so that the abdominal wall provides a firm support for the breathing mechanism. Remember that the easiest and greatest expansion is at the base of the lungs and though expansion is greater at the front it is also possible at the sides and to some extent at the back . . . Inhale to a mental count of five . . . hold for a count of three (without any feeling of strain in the upper chest or neck) . . . by gentle pressure upwards of the diaphragm and contraction of the intercostal muscles, exhale to a light hissing sound . . . 'Don't force it, let it come.' It should be a continuous, even sound. If there is jerkiness or uneven quality of sound, these are caused by diaphragmatic spasms or poor muscular control.

First do breathing exercises in the horizontal position, relaxed, flat on your back. When you have some degree of control in that position, repeat as far as is possible, standing up. At the beginning a little aid to the muscles by the arms is permissible; raising them forwards or sideways for expansion and lowering for contraction. For strengthening the abdominal muscles lie on your back; raise the legs to a position at right angles to the trunk during inhalation (expansion) lowering gradually during exhalation (contraction). Once the principle is established exercises can be invented for further practice; but never forget that the purpose is for the *control of the exhaled breath for the production of voice*, which is dealt with later in this chapter.

A word to the beginner about nervousness would not be amiss. Most good actors are nervous *before* a first night or a first entrance on the stage. It is nerves and not 'nerve' that gives that peculiar extra quality necessary to a good performance. The actor who claims that he is not nervous, means either that he has his nerves under control or is unconsciously admitting that he is lacking in sensitivity. The chair you sit in on the stage has no nerves and is therefore incapable of responding to an audience. The actor can only be faulted if his nervousness is so apparent that it embarrasses the audience. The physical manifestations of nervousness have been dealt with in the foregoing paragraphs. The accomplished actor controls his nerves in order to direct nervous energy into the appropriate artistic channels. There lies the whole point of technique. The technique can be forgotten when it has become subservient to the art and anyone who has reached the stage where he has put his technique behind him will not be reading this book. But even the inexperienced should know that there is a time for practice and a time for performance and the two should be kept in watertight compartments. An actor who gave a second conscious thought to his breathing in front of an audience could never hope to become a good artist. Amateurs without technique often try to find short cuts to be what they consider effective on the stage. One way is to 'work themselves up' for the part or for a particular entrance. They make the mistake of wasting all the energy which should have been held in reserve for the actual entrance, in the dressing-room, in the wings—anywhere but in the right place.

In her fine biography of Edwin Booth, the great American actor, *Prince of Players*, Eleanor Ruggles tells a story of a young actor who eventually became famous:

> . . . In the company was a jolly, eager boy named Otis Skinner, who did Laertes. Every night, during the tedious wait between Laertes' good-bye to Ophelia and his next appearance three acts later when he bounds on to avenge Polonius's death, Skinner would stamp up and down his dressing-room flaying his emotions, and when his cue finally came would hurl himself into the scene. After several nights of this Booth sent for him during the intermission. Booth was smoking as usual and playing solitaire.
>
> "Young man," he said thoughtfully, "I've been watching you and you're killing yourself. You've got some high-tone notion you're supposed to *be* Laertes. Relax! Read a book, write letters, play pinochle. Loaf about in the wings. Don't try to work yourself up, it can't be done. Just wait for your cue, then, when you hear it, *go on the stage and act!*" '

A General Survey of Speech

Speech is a controversial, even an emotional subject, owing to its highly personal nature. Until quite recently a certain manner of speaking was deliberately cultivated and a particular kind of voice was assumed as the hall-mark of social superiority. A saner attitude prevails at present among more intelligent people. The old class-consciousness appears to be giving way to social consciousness. The only real test of good speech for general purposes should be intelligibility. Regional tradition should always be respected but unintelligible speech which is the result of laziness or bad habits is to be deplored anywhere. No one with a sense of history could object to dialect, but anyone with a love of language resents the debasement of language.

The actor is a speech specialist. He must be capable of examining his own speech as well as that of other people, not only unemotionally, but scientifically. If he can speak only in his local accent he must not grumble if he is cast only in local plays. Conversely, if he is limited to neutral speech he will not be surprised if he is not chosen for a part requiring an accent. The qualification of being able to listen and learn has already been mentioned.

It must be said unequivocally that the actor should be able to speak what, for want of a better term is called Standard English, just as it must be said, equally without equivocation, that the broadest regional accent is preferable to an affected accent, which is not to be confused with cultured speech, by which is understood the conforming in some degree to generally accepted standards and the cultivation and improvement of the *natural resources* of voice and speech.

There is a great deal of loose thinking about 'Standard English' or 'Received Pronunciation'. The objectors to it think in terms of 'standardization'. To standardize an individual's speech would be to depersonalize him and it is doubtful whether such a thing is possible even with the advance of medicine and scientific processes such as 'brain-washing'.

If it is allowed that every art has a norm from which the exponent starts, Standard English is the basis of the art of speech. The actor requires a form of spoken English which is more easily understood than any other over a greater area. Slight variants of 'standard' English are inevitable; but it would be difficult to refute the proposition that effective speakers in London, Dublin, Edinburgh, Manchester, Cardiff or even New York, conform to Standard English more than do ineffective speakers in those places. The Yorkshireman who is derisive about the B.B.C. 'accent' will admit on reflection that there is greater similarity between it and what he considers good Yorkshire speech than there is between the B.B.C. accent and the Yorkshire accent which is not approved locally. The fact that locally approved speech in any region approximates to Standard English while that which is disapproved diverges from it is sufficient proof of basic agreement as to the standard. The best speakers from different parts of the country modify their accents for easier intelligibility. The actor has to go further than this. It is not difficult to see that his acting range is enormously increased if he eradicates traces of his native accent, where there is one.

The actor who draws the attention of the audience to the manner rather than the matter of his speech has lost half the battle. We all have mannerisms of speech and gesture which are part of our personalities, but if these obtrude to the extent of getting between actor and audience, the interest of the latter in the character is diminished by the degree of its attention to the actor's mannerisms, and the illusion of the theatre is lost.

DISTINCTNESS $+$ AUDIBILITY $=$ INTELLIGIBILITY

Audibility, by which is meant the carrying power of the voice in the theatre, is mainly dependent on the vowel sounds. Distinctness, meaning the distance at which words are recognizable, depends mainly on the consonants.

People often say they can't hear an actor when they can, in fact, hear him quite well. What they mean is that they can't understand him. So there is no point in being audible if you are indistinct. The sensible actor will ignore the cliché, 'Take care of the consonants and the vowels will look after themselves.' He will learn that even vowel length is determined by the size of the theatre and that speed of delivery is determined mainly by consonants. Only a few of the consonants can be sustained in the same way as most of the vowels. For this reason the vowels are used for exercises in voice production. The vowels *are* the greater part of voice. The consonants are used for making voice into meaningful speech and we use them in articulation exercises.

Sound and Symbol

Knowledge of the phonetic alphabet on the part of all readers cannot be assumed. It would be easier to discuss speech sounds on the printed page if we could work on the principle of one sound one sign. The anomalies of English are well known. There are only twenty-six letters in the alphabet to represent nearly double that number of sounds in the spoken language. There are different spellings of the same sound, e.g. all five vowel *signs* are used to represent one vowel *sound:*

Cabbage; pretty; him; women; busy

apart from combinations of signs representing that same sound:

Carriage; sieve; forfeit; or the double sign, breeches.

Furthermore we have the same sign used for different sounds:

Book and boom; sauce and sausage; butter and butcher.

We are faced with the anomaly, four times as many consonant signs as there are vowel signs in the alphabet, but an almost equal number of vowel and consonant sounds in speech.

Compilers of phonetic alphabets with a separate sign for each sound are limited to Standard English. Attempts at inventing

signs for regional accents and dialect have defeated minds as
great as that of Bernard Shaw. The nearest we can get to a
representation of regional accent, in print, is to describe how
one Standard English vowel is substituted for another. Let us
take two simple sentences, numbering each vowel;

(a) Pa may we all go too   (b) That pen is not much good.
   1   2   3   4   5   6   7   8 9 10 11   12

There we have twelve different sounds subdivided into two
groups, (a) long vowels, (b) short vowels; i.e. Numbers 1 to 6 can
be sustained continuously for as long as we can provide breath
to utter them; numbers 7 to 12 cannot be sustained without
altering the original character of the sound. For example, if
each vowel is sung to a simple scale Number 10 becomes
Number 4 and the word 'not' is changed to 'naught'. (If you
have noticed that 2 and 5 change character when sustained or
sung it means that you have a good ear. This will be dealt with
in later subdivisions of vowel sounds.)

A child reciting 'Rub-a-dub-dub' in S.E. (Standard English)
would use vowel number 11, but a child with a north-country
accent would substitute 12 for 11 and uses the same sound (12)
in 'much' and 'good'. In S.E. the vowel sounds in the last three
words of 'I won one bun' are all the same, i.e.11. But the north-
country child will use 12 in 'won' and 'bun' and 10 in 'one'.

To illustrate substitution of S.E. sounds further we can add
another pair of vowel sounds. No. 13 is repeated in 'her fur',
No. 14 in 'fair hair'. A Belfast child might substitute 13 for 14
saying 'fur her' instead of 'fair hair'. A Tees-side child might
substitute 14 for 13 saying 'hair fair' instead of 'her fur'.

Read the following dialogue with the repetition of S.E. vowel
sound No. 13. Then read it a second time substituting 14 for 13,
imagining a conversation between two workmen, Herb and
Bert, who refer to each other as 'H-air-b' and 'B-air-t'.

> 'Are you workin', Erb?'
> 'Ay, I'm workin', Bert. Where are you workin'?'
> 'Ee, I'm workin' at the blast-furnaces, 'Erb.'
> 'Are you working on the furnace where your father was
> hurt, Bert?'
> 'Ay, but he wasn't hurt badly, Herb. It might have been

Above: 'Julius Caesar' in simple setting. (University College of Swansea Staff Production.)

Below: Interior scene from the University College of Swansea's Staff Production of 'Othello'.

Two exterior scenes from 'Othello'.

Permanent set for 'Othello' with lighting as described in Chapter Seven: interior scenes, stage left; exteriors, stage right.

'Book of the Month', Coleraine Drama Club's production at Portrush Summer Theatre. (*Photo: Sara Jamieson.*)

Above: This improvised curtain setting for 'Pillars of Society' proved effective when a realistic set was impossible. (University College of Swansea Education Department Production.) *Action picture by Victor Hopkins. Below:* Larkfield Training College set for 'Journey's End'; built with filled sandbags and ceiling of stretched black curtain. (*Photo by courtesy of Belfast News-Letter.*)

This lantern is used for following purposes or when a spotlight will have to be handled frequently.

Photographs on this page and following two pages by courtesy of Strand Electric, London.

Left: An iris diaphragm. *Right:* A four-sided adjustable mask which will provide any shape of four-sided beam.

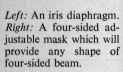

Following spot fitted with a narrow-angle lens.

Above left: There will be cases on a dark stage close to a wing or a cyclorama or other backcloth when light stray must be cut off. To do this a barn-door attachment is clipped to the front and rotated to suit the particular circumstances. *Above right:* This light produces an intense beam variable between spot and flood with soft and indeterminate edges. *Below left:* When the lantern will be required to project a variety of rectangular beam shapes, four independent gate shutters operated by means of external knobs may be fitted. *Below right:* The Junior Spot and the Junior Flood (*illustrated overleaf*) have been designed as complementary lanterns for use on the small stage where very limited money is available.

Above: The Junior Flood provides an efficient wide-angle evenly distributed beam and is ideal for use on the stage itself to provide general wash of light over the acting area or for use on a telescopic stand for lighting door and window backings. The Masking Hood (*left*) which slides into the colour frame runners reduces the beam angle and converts the lantern to a directional unit which can be used to supplement the spotlighting. This accessory is particularly useful in multipurpose halls where general lighting must be provided on the stage for meetings, etc., but more directional lighting is required for dramatic performances. *Below left:* Spotlight mounted on telescopic stand. *Below right:* Colour-change wheel and drive. These accessories fulfil the dual functions of a remotely operated colour-change for stage purposes, and also a continuously rotating colour wheel suitable for dance halls, display work, etc.

worse. He only burnt his shirt in the furnace. It's worth burnin' your shirt to get a few days off workin' at the furnaces, 'Erb.'

To present even this short duologue in the regional accent would be impossible through the medium of print. Further substitutions and modifications of vowels would be necessary as would other characteristics only recognizable through the medium of speech; intonation and rhythm which are the main features of accent, qualities of tone such as nasalization, attack and so on. But it will readily be seen that keen observation and a good ear can be cultivated for a greater appreciation of speech sounds, whether of Standard English or deviations from it.

To conclude the illustrations we shall take a more difficult example, using another sound and attempting four variants of it in spoken English—again bearing in mind the difficulties of showing in print what can really only be heard in speech. Read aloud the sentence.

(5) 'It might be a nice night tonight, Mr. White, mightn't it?'

Isolate the vowel sound in bold type and you will notice that an entirely new feature occurs. (Unless you have already heard it for yourself in Nos. 2 and 5.) Up to the present we have been dealing with *Pure* vowels. That means that the character of the sound is the same throughout and the shape of the mouth is the same at the end as it is at the beginning, i.e. in Standard English. Our latest vowel sound, 15, and 2 and 5 (and to a lesser extent 14) are *Diphthongs*, i.e. a combination of two sounds blended in a subtle way by changing the shape of the mouth at the end from the shape at the beginning of the sound. For instance No. 15 starts with No. 11 (m**u**ch) and changes to No. 9 (**is**). At least that is as near as we can get to a description of the diphthong.

In regional accents the first part of this diphthong is substituted or modified more than is the second half. No. 15, in Cockney, starts with a full-length No. 1 (**Pa**) and finishes with an almost imperceptible No. 9 (**is**). Scottish is difficult; starting with 8 (modified towards 7) and ending with a very shortened 3. Irish (Stage Irish anyway) starts with 10 and ends on 9. If we dare go further and consider Lancashire, for which no symbol exists, but which is half-way between 1 and 7, practise, as follows:

Say No. 1 (**Pa**). With the two little fingers, draw the lips backwards, i.e. altering the elliptical shape of the mouth from the
vertical to the horizontal. Keep the tone going. Let the tongue
fall slightly back in the mouth with a slight raising of it at the
back. Let the soft palate down towards the tongue without
actually touching it. You will notice that the character of the
sound alters and the tone quality become slightly nasalized. The
diphthong ends on a short sound between 3 and 9. It may be a
poor imitation of the Lancashire sound but it is good practice
for examining your power of control over tongue and soft palate,
to say nothing of your tone production.

Your ear will become attuned to differences between the
utterance of vowels in Standard English and regional accent.
The most obvious difference is perhaps the pronunciation of
2 and 5 as diphthongs in the first, and as pure vowels in Northern
England, Scotland, Ireland and Wales.

Sometimes there is a geographical significance demonstrated
by a softer attack in delivery by Southern English speakers and
a harder attack by speakers in Northern England. The two
different kinds of speech are occasionally loosely referred to as
'relaxed' (Southern) and 'tensed' (Northern) but such generalizations are unsatisfactory. There are as many kinds of speech in
the British Isles as there are people living in them. But for the
purpose of study it can be assumed that group differences are
more obvious than the subtleties of individual distinctions.

The terms 'relaxed' and 'tense' have special significance when
applied to speech. The first does not imply flaccidity any more
than the second means strained. Speech would be impossible
without the degree of tonicity which is the result of alternating
states of relaxation and tension in the muscles which control the
speech mechanism. What the actor needs for speech control is
elasticity, or varying degrees of muscular tension in the organs of
articulation: the tongue, the pharynx, lips and cheeks and the
angle of the jaw, in order to produce varying degrees of tone
quality.

A simple analogy may be found in the drumskin, which, if
struck when slackened, produces a dull tone. The tone increases
in brightness as the skin is tightened. We can also think of the
hard palate as a sounding board, like the top of a grand piano.

For further illustration extreme examples of abnormal speech
could be used. A melancholic mental patient, whose muscles are

in a state of flaccidity, might speak in a dull monotonous fashion: a patient in an acute anxiety state, with muscles in a state of excessive tension, might use sharp, piercing, staccato tones. But the inference is not to be drawn from this that extra degrees of tension and relaxation in normal speech have any psychological significance. An actor is primarily interested in the general health of the organs of voice production and articulation.

An examination of Standard English Pure vowels is the next step. Forget about previous numbering of vowel sounds.

BEAD;	BID;	BED;	BAD;	BALM;	BOMB;
1	2	3	4	5	6
BOUGHT;		BOOK;	BOOM;	(FURTHER;	BUD)
7		8	9	10 11	12

(Ignore 10, 11 and 12.) Nos. 1 and 9 are 'tense' vowels, the muscular tension being greater in the tongue in 1; and greater in the lip and cheek muscles in 9. No. 5, however, is a 'lax' vowel, i.e. the muscles of the organs of articulation are generally more relaxed than they are for 1 and 9.

When your doctor wants to examine your throat he asks you to say 'AH' because the mouth is more open on this sound than on any other. The aperture between the upper and lower teeth is greater, the soft palate is higher, the tongue lower and consequently the throat is more open and visible. If you compare the size of the resonating chamber of the mouth in 'AH' with that of 'EE' where the tongue is raised nearer to the hard palate and the aperture between the teeth is smaller, you will see that the volume, and even the pitch of the vowels, is affected by the size and shape of the instrument.

If the vowels 1 to 9 are practised (not the words), it will be noticed that muscular tension decreases gradually from 1 to 5 as the aperture between the teeth increases and the mouth becomes more open; and that tension increases from 5 to 9 as the aperture for emission of sound between the lips decreases.

Say: 'EE', 'AH', 'OO'.

Notice the change in the shape, externally first, for lips only:

'EE': narrow horizontal eliptical; 'AH': wide vertical eliptical; 'OO': Small, rounded, puckered.

Practise this combination of sounds over and over again. It is important to remember that extra tenseness must not be added to the natural tenseness of 'EE' and 'OO'. This is a mistake often made in carrying out exercises which defeats their purpose. The muscles must always be as relaxed as the character of the sound will allow. Furthermore, the lips must not be forced open to their fullest capacity on 'AH'. This again produces tensions on a relaxed sound. Opening the mouth too wide has the effect of closing the throat and you can see for yourself the faucal muscles of the throat tighten as you force the lips apart. This is another common mistake. The open (or relaxed) throat is more conducive to good voice than the open mouth. There is no contradiction here: gently does it!

It will be noticed that only four of the nine vowels are long vowels: sounds which can be sustained on a single breath.

Say each of them on a single breath: 'EE', 'AH', 'AW', 'OO'. Then intone each for as long as you can increase the tone. Think of two points only; the diaphragm and the lips, *not* the throat! A vowel is a *free*, *open* sound, modified by, but not obstructed by the organs of articulation. Think in terms of *forward tone*; the column of air from the base of the lungs to its emission as voice. Don't chew it or swallow it! The more forward you can get it the greater the amplification and the purer the tone. When you get it to the lips, give it an extra 'follow-through' as if you were directing it to the back of a theatre.

Now intone all four continuously on a single breath, with a slow mental count of two on each; i.e. a slow count of eight:

'EE-AH-AW-OO'

Take a deep breath and using residual as well as inhaled air—this means the use of the 'Abdominal Press' in addition to inter-costal diaphragmatic control—but stopping before you have reached your limit, or before volume begins to decrease or the tone begins to fall back; and intone:

'EE-AH-AW-OO-EE-AH-AW-OO-EE-AH-AW-OO-EE-AH-AW-OO-EE-AH-AW-OO.'

Repeat with the addition of vowel No. 10, 'UR' (first syllable in **FURTHER**)

'EE-UR-AH-AW-OO-EE-UR-AH-AW-OO-EE-UR-AH-
AW-OO-EE-UR-AH, etc.'

You must be careful not to effect any change in the shape of the mouth during phonation of a pure vowel, or it becomes 'diphthongized', e.g. many 'Cockneyisms' are the result of substituting a double for a single vowel; No. 1 'EE' is preceded by No. 11 or the second syllable in 'FURTHER' so that we hear something like 'A cup of "T-ER-EE".' (The neutral vowel plus "EE".)

Before leaving pure vowels, i.e. those with no organic or acoustic change, a few words about the neutral vowel would not be amiss, as this is the sound most frequently used in English speech. We hear it in the definite and indefinite articles when unstressed: The man, a dog; and in the final syllable of words such as, further, actor, sulphur; or trespass, tortoise, portrait, though the use of a diphthong is common in the last two. It can be represented by any vowel signs as in the following sentences.

'I had had about enough long ago, and as I saw another man arrive, I hoped that that was the end of the thing.'
'Are you content with the contents?' 'From here but not to there.'

This sound is used more in colloquial than in formal speech. To use it too little is pedantic; to use it too much is slovenly. Its over-use can reduce intelligibility, especially in the large theatre.

For practice of the diphthongs, lists of monosyllabic words can be made containing the first and second elements of the compound vowels in 'mine', 'town' and 'coin', e.g.:

$$
\begin{aligned}
\text{fine} &= \textbf{fun} + \textbf{fin} \\
\text{pout} &= \textbf{pun} + \textbf{put} \\
\text{boil} &= \textbf{bog} + \textbf{bill}
\end{aligned}
$$

Since a diphthong is a combination of two short vowels which cannot be sustained, we can, for practice only, substitute the nearest equivalent long vowel for intoning for voice practice, giving equal length to each half of the sound as follows:

fine = **farm** + **seen**
pout = **palm** + **boot**
boil = **ball** + **weal**

One full diphthong not yet mentioned can be heard in the second of the following pairs of words; the vowel in the first is a pure vowel: June, dune; jew, duke; yew, few; coo, cue; two, tune; do, due; moon, immune.

Then there are the 'murmur' diphthongs; simply a pure vowel followed by the neutral vowel, as in:

peer	poor	pore	pair
leer	lure	lore	lair
dear	dour	door	dare
mere	moor	more	mare
shear	sure	shore	share
beer	boor	bore	bare

The list is given for the benefit of those people who may otherwise speak Standard English but who pronounce 'pore' as 'paw', 'lore' as 'law', 'floor' as 'flaw', 'saw' as 'sore', or vice versa.

There are also triphthongs, i.e. a diphthong plus the neutral vowel, as in 'flower' and 'fire', pronounced by many people with one sound in the vowel part instead of a blending of three, e.g. 'flah' and 'fah'.

Confusion arises among some people who should know better, between the pure vowel and the murmur diphthongs, because of the 'intrusive "R" '. One hears 'the "paw(r)" of the dog'. 'It is the law(r) in Australia(r) and Africa(r) and China(r), and India(r) also' is not yet accepted as good spoken English even by those who condemn pedantic speech and might accept 'The idea(r) of it.'

The Consonants

Although consonantal sounds are produced by some form of obstruction in the breath stream by the organs of articulation, it is incorrect, from the point of view of tonal quality, to think in terms of a definite line of demarcation between vowels and consonants. For example, more voice can be produced on a voiced continuant consonant than on a stopped (or short) vowel. Some consonants are better for voice production exercises than are some of the vowels, e.g. 'M', 'N', 'NG'. These three are 'nasals' and provide overtones of resonance in the nasal cavities and pharynx. (We must be careful to distinguish between the nasal resonance of these sounds and the unpleasant general nasalization of speech.) The approximation of the lips in 'M'; the blade of the tongue and the front of the hard palate in 'N'; and the back of the tongue and the soft palate in 'NG', prevents emission of tone through the mouth and directs it to the nasal cavities. Exercises for nasal resonance are worth practising for extra tone quality.

Say: 'M-N-NG; M-N-NG; M-N-NG; M-N-NG; M-N-NG; M-N-NG.'

Repeat, preceding with different vowel sounds: 'IM-IN-ING; IM-IN-ING; IM-IN-ING; IM-IN-ING; IM-IN-ING.'

Repeat, directing the tone as far forward as the obstruction on each consonant permits: do not press the lips tightly together on 'M', keep them relaxed enough for maximum vibration so that you feel a tingling sensation. Produce the same sensation in the front of the face at the top of the nose on 'N' and 'NG'. This time prolong the 'M', 'N' and 'NG' increasing the tone.

'OM-ON-ONG; OMM-ONN-ONGNG; OMMM-ONNN-ONGNGNG . . .'

Make up exercises for sustaining the tone on liquid 'L' and trilled 'R'. Remember that these are 'con-*sonants*', subjoining vowel sounds, and the better the con-sonant the better the sonant qualities of the vowel.

Some of the consonants are made without voice, with breath alone, but these have voiced equivalents, with the articulatory organs in the same position:

Unvoiced:	p	t	k	f	s	th	sh;	(6) **th**in (7) **sh**y
	1	2	3	4	5	6	7	
Voiced:	b	d	g	v	z	dh	zh;	(6) **th**y (7) a**z**ure

1, 2 and 3 are 'stopped': 4, 5, 6 and 7 are prolongable.

Exercises should be practised for accuracy of contact of the organs of articulation used to produce the consonants, first with the unvoiced and next with voiced sounds:

> **P**it-a-**p**at-a-**p**it-a-**p**at-a-**p**it-a-**p**at-a-**p**it . . .
>   (hitting the 'p' hard.)
> Pi**t**-a-pa**t**-a-pi**t**-a-pa**t**-a-pi**t**-a-pa**t**-a-pi**t** . . .
>   (hitting the 't' hard.)

Combinations of 'voiced-stopped' and 'nasals' are excellent for improvement of tone quality:

> **Din**-a-den-a-**din**-a-den-a-**din**-a-den-a-**din** . . .
> Din-a-**den**-a-din-a-**den**-a-din-a-**den**-a-din . . .
> Di**nnnn**-a-de**nnnn**-a-di**nnnnn**-a-de**nnnnnn**-a-di**nnnnnn**-a-de**nnnnnn** . . .
> **Bim**-a-boom-a-**bim**-a-boom-a-**bim**-a-boom-a-**bim** . . .
> Bim-a-**boom**-a-bim-a-**boom**-a-bim-a-**boom**-a-bim . . .
> Bi**mmm**-a-boo**mmm**-a-bi**mmmm**-a-boo**mmmm**-a-bi**mmmmm**-a-boo**mmmmm** . . .

The commonest peculiarities in articulation of consonants are 'substitution' and 'assimilation'. In the first we substitute a weaker for a stronger sound, or an unvoiced for a voiced sound. For example, we may say 'su**p**stitute', sacrificing the voice on 'b' for the breath on 'p'. This amounts to little on one word but if you speak 10,000 words in an hour and estimate the sacrifice of the 'su**p**stance' for the shadow, or voice for breath, you may be surprised at the loss of intelligibility.

'Assimilation' is legitimate in many cases. We do not refer to a 'cu**p**board'; the weaker sound has been, by common usage, assimilated by the stronger, and we say, 'cu(p)board'. There are, however, examples of common usage which are not yet acceptable in the theatre (except in character parts), for instance, although it is easier to say 'gimme' than 'give me', because of the assimilation of the weaker 'v' by the stronger 'm', we must make the effort to say both sounds on the stage. 'Isn't it?' is sufficiently abbreviated without the still further curtailment to 'I'n i'?' We hear this kind of slovenly speech from people without any trace of accent. They think they are saying 'A pair of gloves', when what they are really saying is 'dloves'. '**G**' is made by the approximation of the back of the tongue with the soft palate; 'd' by the tip of the tongue with the teeth ridge. '**Gl** . . .' is too athletic a

feat of articulation; some people cannot do it without the inter-
polation of a neutral vowel between the 'g' and the 'l'. Actors
must practise difficult combinations of sounds and not take the
line of least resistance allowed non-professional speakers.

Good speech can be acquired only by attention to detail,
which requires ear training. The reader must apply himself
diligently to material outside the scope of this book, e.g. that
sounds are modified by those which precede or follow them.
The long vowel 'EE' is longer before a voiced consonant than
it is before its unvoiced equivalent; in 'bead' than in 'beat'; in
'leave' than in 'leaf'; in 'seize' that in 'cease'. Notice the modification in the diphthong in the following pairs of words; tide, tight;
cries, thrice; tiger, like; imbibe, pipe. These characteristics may
be of little consequence in colloquial drama but subtle distinctions of sound values must be observed for effective speaking in
poetic drama.

Once the principles of voice and speech practice has been
established the student will be able to invent or find exercises
for himself and there is space only for two more suggestions.
For vowel practice: 'The Lady of Shalott' (Tennyson) has nine-
teen nine-line stanzas, each with first four, followed by three
end-of-line rhymes. This is excellent for repetition of most of the
vowels.

In London recently a course for businessmen was organized.
The object was apparently to sell more detergents, to win friends
and influence people, and to sell more spin-driers. Part
of the course consisted of gibberish, making unintelligible vocal
noises. The result is one of conjecture as far as sales are concerned but as a loosening-up exercise for the organs of articulation it could do no harm. The more things change the more
they stay as they are! The 'hip-bath, hip-bath, hip-bath' and
how now brown cow' of the old-fashioned elocution books
appear as cold logic by comparison with sales-talk gibberish
and the 'method' school's serious request to imagine yourself a
typewriter or a lawn-mower.

Some reliable books on voice and speech can be picked up on
the second-hand bookstalls for a few coppers. Millard's *Grammar
of Elocution* can be found almost any day of the week for three-
pence or sixpence. It was published about eighty years ago.
Our knowledge of the principles of speech has not altered very
greatly in that time and Millard packed it with first-rate exer-

cises. To illustrate this point further we shall end this chapter with an exercise from a book published fifty years ago, with pictures of gentlemen in top-hats and frock-coats, schoolboys in knickerbockers, women in bloomers, mouth-stretching exercises and facial gymnastics complete with *pince-nez*.

For consonant practice: (from *Voice and its Natural Development* by Herbert Jennings.)

The following exercises for articulation and syllabification should be read through:

1. SILENTLY: For determination of stress and phrasing.
2. On half-voice.
3. On full voice.
4. To a whisper.
5. SILENTLY, with exaggerated placing and shaping of tongue and lips.

The ineligibility of the preliminaries is unparalleled.

Such individual irregularities are generally irremediable.

He acted contrarily to the peremptory injunctions.

We alienate many by requiting a few with supernumerary gratuities.

An inalienable eligibility of election which was of an authority which could not be disputed rendered the interposition of his friends altogether supererogatory.

In promulgating your esoteric cogitations, or articulating your superficial sentimentalities, and amicable philosophical or psychological observations, beware of platitudinous ponderosity.

Let your conversational communications possess a clarified conciseness, a compacted comprehensibility, coalescent consistency, and a concatenated cogency.

Eschew all conglomerations of flatulent garrulity, jejune babblement, and asinine affections.

Let your extemporaneous descantings and unpremeditated expatiations have intelligibility and veracious vivacity without rhodomontade or thrasonical bombast. Sedulously avoid all polysyllabic profundity, pompous prolixity, psittaceous vacuity, ventriloquial verbosity, and vaniloquent vapidity. In other words, talking plainly, briefly, naturally, sensibly, truthfully. Keep from slang; don't put on airs; say what you mean, mean what you say; and *don't use big words*.

CHAPTER SIX

Voice modulation; rhythm and phrasing

THE cultivation of sensitivity and perception of meaning must go hand in hand with the pure mechanics of voice and speech. Where it does not increase awareness of the underlying idea of the words, speech remains, at the worst, unintelligible sound, or at best, half-realized communication. The actor must have complete accord of sound and sense. He should be able to modulate his voice and colour the tone so that it is in sympathy with the emotional content of the subject matter.

Modulation is a combination of PITCH, PACE, PAUSE and POWER. Remembering again the exception to the rule, a higher pitch of voice is usually associated with a quicker rate of delivery and a lower pitch with a slower rate. A child knows instinctively the vocal reactions to the excitement of a football match or the anger of a quarrel, and the solemnity of a funeral or the reverence expected of him in church. Sadness is usually expressed in lower and slower speech; gladness in higher and quicker speech. While it would not be correct to say that the principle is applied throughout a tragedy or a comedy, the key in which each is pitched is not dissimilar.

The pause has several purposes: the breath pause to provide the raw material for the following sentence of phrase; the pause to allow the audience to assimilate what has been said; the emphatic pause and the dramatic pause to heighten significance, to change the mood or the pace, to produce the element of surprise, for 'timing' in comedy and for increasing intensity in tragedy.

Power is like controlling the stops of an organ, for increasing or decreasing loudness or volume and intensity and for dramatic effect. The actor has to be audible at the back of the theatre on a whisper and agreeably intelligible to the front row when he is shouting.

Rhythm and Phrasing are integral parts of modulation and are inseparable for the purpose of speech. Rhythm is an indefinable quality. It cannot be measured with a metronome; it is

91

as different from metre as the lapping of the sea on the sand is from the 'chug-chug-chug' of an engine. In verse the strict adherence to the metre produces doggerel. Rhythm in poetry is produced by substitutions and inversions, and irregularities to the basic metrical form. In speech the regular repetition of the same qualities and quantities of sound would be inhuman and impossible but occasionally we have the impression that this is what is happening; the speaker is monotonous and after listening for a time we lose the sense and are conscious only of the sound. Rhythmic speech is a pattern of irregular upward and downward curves of the voice. The difference between speech and song is that in the first there is an immeasurable glide from one note to another and in the second there is a measurable leap. We are familiar with the popular singer with the wide appeal to the non-musical because of his ability to compromise between the two, by 'slurring' from one note to another.

Phrasing is determined by the sense in speech and not by punctuation as in silent reading; by the ear, not the eye. A phrase is spoken on a single breath and can be separated from other phrases by a pause or suspension of voice. The sense can be complete or subordinate to the general sense of the passage spoken. Good punctuation can be a guide. It has been said that in Shakespeare the pause is indicated by a count of one for a comma, two for a semi-colon, three for a colon and four for a full-stop, though this cannot be taken as entirely satisfactory for interpretation in view of differences in punctuation from edition to edition.

The intending actor could start practice by reading aloud for a given period every day. He can begin with factual material or taking the leading article of a good newspaper. Subject matter of an objective nature is good for exercising the articulative organs and strengthening the middle register of the voice, i.e. that which is used for everyday purposes. From objective the student can gradually work into material of a more subjective nature, to characters and situations with which he can identify himself. Fairly long passages are better for helping the beginner to feel the atmosphere. One man's meat is another man's poison and the choice depends largely on the temperament of the individual, though later on, acquired technique will help to overcome personal prejudice. For example, one person may like Dickens and have a copy of the work as arranged by Emlyn

Williams for the Dickens readings in which he toured widely.
The reader may enjoy reading of the birth and death of Paul,
from *Dombey and Son*. Another person might think there was
too much caricature and sentimentality for his taste or be out of
sympathy generally with Dickens. There is another Paul for him.
He might find greater subtlety and true sentiment in D. H.
Lawrence's Paul in *Sons and Lovers* and might enjoy reading
aloud Chapter Four; The Young Life of Paul. He would be a
limited actor who could find no sympathy for either Paul. Then
there is a wide selection of short stories with plenty of action,
dialogue, description and climax which are all part of drama.
From there the reader could progress to speeches of single
characters which are fairly complete in themselves. Two of the
longest speeches in modern drama are the Inquisitor's speech
from Scene Four of *Saint Joan* (Bernard Shaw) and Becket's
Christmas morning sermon from *Murder in the Cathedral* (T. S.
Eliot)—to say nothing of the speeches of the Knights towards
the end of the same play. An actress could try three speeches of
St Joan for change of mood and development of character,
commencing 'Ah! if, if, if! If if's and an's were pots and pans
there'd be no need of tinkers.' 'Where would you all have been
now if I had heeded that sort of truth' and 'Yes: they told me
you were fools . . .' on pages 134, 138 and 165 of the Penguin
edition. In addition, a repertoire of monologues could be built
up. A man could collect passages like Tchekhov's *'On the
Harmfulness of Tobacco'* and a woman Strindberg's *The
Stronger* although this is much longer and more difficult. But
these selections are suggested for practice and working alone.
They are mentioned because they are all to be found in any
public library and no expense need be involved. It is a beginning.
The student actor eventually finds ways and means of providing
material for practice.

At the same time, the student will require exercises of a more
systematic kind, shorter selections for repetition and easier
control, to use concurrently with his longer and changing
selections. Those already mentioned are all in prose and it has
to be remembered that poetic drama is becoming increasingly
popular with the better dramatic societies. An ability to speak
prose does not qualify an actor for the speaking of poetry but
an actor who cannot speak poetry never realizes his capacity
for speaking prose. Verse speaking would be worth the time

given to practice if only for the experience of expressing greater ideas in fewer words. It provides opportunities for heightened emotion with economy of speech; an intensity of feeling rarely afforded by colloquial speech without appearing 'ham'. For the novice it has a form and shape which can be seen and felt, more easily than the so-called 'style' of prose.

In the practice of exercises for modulation of the voice, control of pace should be mastered first, then pitch, followed by power. Pause can be left until the dramatic element is added. It is easier to run than to walk gracefully and it is easier to speak quickly than it is to speak slowly and eloquently. How many words a minute do you speak ordinarily? How do you vary the rate of your delivery? You've never given it a thought? You will have to give it considerable thought if you are going on the stage. How quickly do you sight-read? The counsel for the defence in the case of *Lady Chatterley's Lover* is reported as having claimed that the average rate of silent reading is two hundred words a minute. If, as is the case, an actor in quick comedy or farce speaks at that rate on the stage, you may be surprised to learn that some people speak as quickly as others read. But to speak intelligibly at that speed on the stage calls for hard practice. The following exercises are designed for you to find out for yourself how slowly you can speak without sacrificing sense and vitality and how quickly you can speak without speech becoming meaningless gabble.

Each of the exercises contains one hundred words. Two of them are speeches written to be spoken by actors on the stage. They are offered for a comparison of the speaking of:

1. Lyric poetry.
2. Literary prose.
3. Dramatic verse.
4. Colloquial speech.

Compare the application of modulation, between verse and prose, then between content and form. Read the more literary 1 and 2 first. There is measured tread in both but there is a personal quality of 'emotion recollected in tranquillity' about the first. The second has grandeur but it is didactic, the questions are rhetorical; you are not being asked, you are being told. Yet both come into the same category so far as modulation goes.

slow pace and low pitch, without any great variation of either. Notice the arrangement and choice of vowels, especially of long vowels in the Yeats poem: 'old and grey', 'glowing bars'. The lyric will perhaps take a few seconds longer than the prose because of the content and the form, just under the minute, but certainly not fewer than forty-five seconds, that is, to be anywhere near a true interpretation.

1. *When you are old and grey and full of sleep,*
   And nodding by the fire, take down this book,
   And slowly read, and dream of the soft look
   Your eyes had once, and of their shadows deep;

   How many loved your moments of glad grace,
   And loved your beauty with love false or true,
   But one man loved the pilgrim soul in you,
   And loved the sorrows of your changing face;

   And bending down beside the glowing bars,
   Murmur, a little sadly, how love fled
   And paced upon the mountains overhead
   And hid his face amid a crowd of stars.

   (W. B. YEATS.)

2. The dust of great persons' graves is speechless too, it sayes nothing, it distinguishes nothing: As soon the dust of a wretch whom thou wouldest not, as of a Prince whom thou couldest not look upon, will trouble thine eyes, if the wind blow it thither: and when a whirle-winde hath blowne the dust of the Church-yard into the Church, and the man sweeps out the dust of the Church into the Church-yard, who will undertake to sift those dusts again, and to pronounce, This is the Patrician, the noble flowre, and this is the yeomanly, this the Plebeian bran.

(From a sermon by JOHN DONNE)

Now let us take two highly dramatic speeches, vastly different from the first two and quite different from each other.

3. *Paulina:*

'. . . . The Queen? . . .
I say she's dead: I'll swear't: if word nor oath
Prevail not, go and see. If you can bring
Tincture of lustre in her lip, her eye.
Heat outwardly, or breath within, I'll serve you
As I would do the gods. But, O thou tyrant!
Do not repent these things, for they are heavier
Than all thy woes can stir; therefore betake thee
To nothing but despair. A thousand knees
Ten thousand years together, naked, fasting
Upon a barren mountain, and still winter
In storm perpetual, could not move the gods
To look what way thou wert.

(SHAKESPEARE'S *Winter's Tale*)

4. *Myra:* Don't drive so fast. You know I hate it on this
cliff road . . . I said not so fast . . . I shall learn to drive myself,
that's all . . . You're behaving very stupidly. If you go on like
this everyone'll see something's wrong . . . If you think you'll
goad me into leaving you, you won't . . . Not that you mean a
thing to me, I've always despised you . . . but to me you mean
security—at least your money does—and I'm not going to
let that go. Understand? . . . So you'd better make the best of
things . . . What's the matter? What are you stopping for?

(From *The Tunnel*, a radio play by MABEL CONSTAN-
DUROS and HOWARD AGG. Myra's last words before
Denis murders her.)

It doesn't matter that they are both women's speeches. They
could equally be men's for the purpose of practice. Paulina's
speech will take about the same time as the Yeats' poem but
Myra's will take only half the time.

If that surprises you consider the form and the content. *The
Winter's Tale* is blank verse; *The Tunnel* the quick-fire of modern
everyday speech. Paulina is lying. The Queen is not dead and
she knows it. She is talking to the King, who, in the madness of
jealousy, accused his wife of infidelity and sentenced her to death
He realized her innocence, as he believed, too late. Now he is

stricken with remorse and repentance and is on his knees, begging forgiveness. Paulina has protested the Queen's innocence from the beginning and contrives to save her from death and have her hidden. She knows that the King and Queen are eventually to be reunited but she is determined that he shall suffer for the wrong he has perpetrated on his faithful wife. She is angry but it is with a slow, deliberate, burning passion that she twists the knife of vengeance in the open wound.

Paulina's speech can be used as an exercise in 'producing' a speech for yourself, in the absence of a producer. The rate of delivery will alternate between slow deliberation—slower even in some phrases than the lyric poem of Yeats—and quick articulation as rapid as the fastest phrases of Myra in *The Tunnel*. You can run the whole gamut of your range of pitch and use the pause for dramatic effect. You will also require a great deal of power for the climax towards the end.

'I say she's dead' (every word deliberately), 'I'll swear't' (quickly, as if to give seeming truth to the lie and convince even herself momentarily), 'If word nor oath prevail not, go and see' ('word' relating to 'say' and 'oath' relating to 'swear' call for mixed intonation which will lengthen the vowel in each, but get the speed necessary for defiance on 'Go and see'). Speed up on 'If you can . . . or breath within'—pause—then slow down for 'I'll serve you . . . gods'—long pause—'But O thou tyrant' (hang on to the two long vowels so that this is the slowest and most venomous phrase in the speech). Slight pause. 'Do not repent these things' (spit this out rapidly) 'For they . . . can stir' (slowly and mercilessly), 'Therefore betake . . . despair' (rapidly and ruthlessly), 'A thousand knees . . . storm perpetual' (this is the climax and if possible, take it all on one breath, rising in volume and increasing in speed) 'Could not . . . thou wert' (slow down gradually from beginning to end of this phrase with quiet, passionate intensity).

That is one interpretation. There are others. But it is worth working at a specific presentation if only for the discipline which you may be asked to bring to a part in a play by your producer. When you think you have practised Paulina's speech to a standard satisfactory to yourself, in the manner suggested, experiment with it in your own way by different applications of modulation.

The selection from *The Tunnel* shows the turning of the worm.

The husband cannot stand his wife's treatment of him any longer. You can imagine him stopping the car suddenly at the edge of a cliff, leaving the brake off, leaping out and pushing the car over the edge before Myra realizes that she is being murdered.

Myra's speech requires very little variation in pace and pitch, unless for the terror at the end when she realizes what is happening. It is the rapid, near staccato delivery of the neurotic, nagging wife. At the same time, monotony must be avoided, as in the lyric poem. The Shakespeare selection offers the greatest range of modulation. Vowel tone and resonance will see you through 1 and 2; neat, firm articulation of the consonants is necessary for the speed demanded of 4; 3 requires both. The four selections provide you with a sound exercise for testing and improving the modulation of your voice.

There you have a four hundred word exercise lasting approximately three minutes, when you are able to do the first and the third in about fifty seconds and the last one in about twenty-five.

When you can manage some degree of control of voice and speech in formal exercises such as those just given, try out the principles of modulation with speeches you are familiar with. Do not be content with one interpretation and be prepared even to experiment with several ways of delivering the same speech. For example, take a couple of Shylock's speeches from *The Merchant of Venice*; 'Signor Antonio, many a time and oft . . .' (Act I scene iii) and 'To bait fish withal: if it will feed nothing else, it will feed my revenge.' (Act III, scene i.) They are both about two hundred words long; set yourself the task of speaking the first speech at the rate of *one* hundred words a minute, i.e. about two minutes. Although you may find this too slow for a dramatic interpretation, it can be taken at this speed without completely sacrificing the sense. Then do the second speech at the rate of *two* hundred words a minute, i.e. about one minute. This is very quick and does not allow for the necessary dramatic pauses. But at least you will have tried out the extremes of relaxed and tensed speech. If you do both speeches again, allowing for greater variations of modulation in each, you will find that the basic speeds are not vastly different from the experimental approach. Then try out a monologue, preferably in verse for easier control and demanding some characterization, e.g.

Browning's *My Last Duchess* has just over five-hundred words. The Duke who makes the speech is elegant, cold and cruel, and any passion is implied in the words but controlled in the delivery. He is speaking to an inferior, the emissary of another nobleman, who has come to discuss the dowry to be paid on the marriage of his master's daughter with the Duke, who has pitilessly murdered his last duchess out of pride and jealousy. The speech requires no histrionics. Take it at your own speed—which is— what? Three-and-a-half to four minutes for five hundred words? A hundred and twenty-five or a hundred and fifty words a minute? Have you found out anything about your voice and speech by now? If so, you are discovering yourself and you are on the way to becoming an actor.

If you have gone to the trouble of borrowing a collection of Browning's poems from the library (if you haven't one already) use some of them for practising rhythm in speaking. The rhythms are obvious but are no worse for that at this stage. Browning was a good craftsman and if it sounds 'um-ti-tiddy, um-ti-tiddy' that's your fault, not his. Don't be put off Browning because of a little unfashionable optimism. There are probably poets who have more to say but it is a pity that some of the minor moderns can't make what they have to say clear enough for the purpose of reading aloud. Get down to the practice and leave the philosophy till later. Read aloud Browning's 'Up at a Villa—Down in the City', 'A Toccata of Galuppi's', 'Love among the Ruins', 'De Gustibus——' and others which you think lend themselves to speaking. You might even enjoy Rudyard Kipling for practising strong rhythms. Borrow *The Definitive Edition of Rudyard Kipling's Verse* from the library. Look up the contents and you will find a dozen titles beginning 'Ballad of . . .' and a couple of dozen beginning 'Song of . . .'. There are some good dramatic pieces, e.g. 'The Roman Centurion's Song', 'The Looking Glass', or 'The Truce of the Bear'—really strong meat this last! If you are too sophisticated for strong meat you might consider rhythms like:

> *You have heard the beat of the off-shore wind,*
> *And the thresh of the deep-sea rain;*
> *You have heard the song—how long? how long?*
> *Pull out on the trail again.*
>
> (From 'The Long Trail')

or

> *Who hath desired the Sea?—the immense and*
>   *contemptuous surges?*
> *The shudder, the stumble, the swerve, as the*
>   *star-stabbing bowsprit emerges?*
> (From 'The Sea and the Hills')

You'll have none of it? It is good enough for T. S. Eliot!

Do you remember the poems you did at school? You probably hated them for one of two reasons, (*a*) you didn't know what they were about, or, (*b*) the teacher showed the whites of his eyes when he droned them out as if he was at a prayer meeting. You probably liked some of them for the wrong reasons. Perhaps you actually remember some of the more immature ones and you still enjoy quoting—the parody:

> *The road was a rasher of bacon,*
> *The moon was a scrambled egg,*
> *And the highwayman came riding, riding, riding . . .*

but you gave up reading that 'kid-stuff' when you put school behind you and entered the big real adult world. Does that mean that the world of poetry is the opposite? Small? Unreal? Childish? If you take another look at some of those poems now you may discover that your dislike and lack of understanding of them was because at the time they were too 'big', too 'real', too 'adult'. Have you ever tried reading aloud the Bible, Milton, *Pilgrim's Progress*? Dull? Oh no! Just *too* adult! Go back to those school poems and see what you missed.

First take a couple which you read in the junior school and secondly, a couple of sonnets you read in the senior school. The first two are almost the same length, just under three-hundred words. Number one is a lyric-ballad, an allegory, a story told with the maximum of economy and perfect choice of words; it is a poem for two voices; question (the first three stanzas) and answer (the rest). It's dramatic; it's tragic; it has almost a 'cloying' beauty, to use a word Keats loved. Furthermore it has a climax and anti-climax in juxtaposition in the penultimate stanza which amounts to genius.

This time you shall not be asked to go to the library. We shall

print all four in full for you since you might not take our word
about those school poems.

> *Oh what can ail thee, knight-at-arms,*
>   *Alone and palely loitering?*
> *The sedge has wither'd from the lake,*
>   *And no birds sing.*
>
> *O what can ail thee, knight-at-arms,*
>   *So haggard and so woe-begone?*
> *The squirrel's granary is full*
>   *And the harvest's done.*
>
> *I see a lily on thy brow*
>   *With anguish moist and fever dew,*
> *And on thy cheek a fading rose*
>   *Fast withereth too.*
>
> *I met a lady in the meads,*
>   *Full beautiful—a faery's child,*
> *Her hair was long, her foot was light,*
>   *And her eyes were wild.*
>
> *I made a garland for her head,*
>   *And bracelets too, and fragrant zone*
> *She looked at me as she did love*
>   *And made sweet moan.*
>
> *I set her on my pacing steed*
>   *And nothing else saw all day long,*
> *For sidelong would she lean, and sing*
>   *A faery's song.*
>
> *She found me roots of relish sweet,*
>   *And honey wild and manna dew,*
> *And sure in language strange she said,*
>   *'I love thee true.'*
>
> *She took me to her elfin grot,*
>   *And there she wept and sighed full sore,*
> *And there I shut her wild, wild eyes*
>   *With kisses four.*

And there she lulled me asleep,
And there I dreamed—Ah! woe betide:
The latest dream I ever dream'd
On the cold hill side.

I saw pale kings and princes too
Pale warriors, death-pale were they all:
They cried—'La belle dame sans merci
Hath thee in thrall!'

I saw their starved lips in the gloam
With horrid warning gaped wide:
And I awoke and found me here,
On the cold hill side.

And this is why I sojourn here,
Alone and palely loitering,
Though the sedge is wither'd from the lake
And no birds sing.

(KEATS)

What is it about? What do you want it to be about? Then that is what it is about. Life and death, love and lust, good and evil, joy and grief, idealism and disillusion, innocence and corruption, wonder and despair; there is a terrible, awful beauty which attracts and repels. So—it's a child's poem! Do you remember when you thought that beauty was the fairies at the bottom of your garden? Something you never saw? But you see it now, in this poem. If you don't, let us continue with the technique; you'll need it all.

Now read the poem . . . and again . . . How long did it take you? Not less than three minutes? If it did read it again. Remember those long vowels, the steady delivery, the compassionate, patient inquiry of the first three stanzas, the forlorn inexorability of retrospect, the remembrance of ecstasy changing to nightmarish realization at the climax in the narrative. All the intensity, the rejection, the bitter-sweet of a first experience of youth is in this little gem of drama of fewer than three hundred words. There is no excuse for monotony of delivery. There is movement and pace and anticipation in a line like 'I set her on my pacing steed' and the savouring, the dwelling on the object of adoration in the following line, 'and nothing else saw all day long'; the same kind of treatment, as a variation on a given theme, in the first two lines of the stanza next but one. Give the climax pace and resonance and tone colour. For the six lines of the anti-climax, drain the voice of colour and vitality. The prospect is flat, hopeless, dead. There is nothing but awakening on a cold hill and the withered sedge and no bird-song. The hot blood has frozen.

Take no notice of your bookish friends who are horrified at this treatment of Keats and tell you that 'the poet must be allowed to speak for himself', as though his poems had been buried with him and were just as lifeless. Tell them you are training to be an actor in a theatre—not a medium at a séance!

If you read *Alice in Wonderland* as a child you would have to read it again as an adult to appreciate its significance to the full. It contains a poem of equal length to the Keats' poem. It is not by any means great poetry, but it is great fun and provides an opportunity of comparing the technique of speech in comedy with that of the other extreme as illustrated in 'La Belle Dame . . .' It says in a light-hearted way that there is nothing so boring to the old as the curiosity of the young and that there is nothing as old-fashioned or as intolerant as youth—among other things.

'You are old, Father William,' the young man said
'And your hair has become very white;
And yet you incessantly stand on your head—
Do you think, at your age, it is right?'

'In my youth,' Father William replied to his son,
'I feared it might injure the brain;
But, now that I'm perfectly sure I have none,
Why, I do it again and again.'

'You are old,' said the youth, 'As I mentioned before.
And have grown most uncommonly fat;
Yet you turned a back-somersault in at the door—
Pray, what is the reason of that?'

'In my youth,' said the sage, as he shook his grey locks,
'I kept all my limbs very supple
By the use of this ointment—one shilling the box—
Allow me to sell you a couple?'

'*You are old,*' *said the youth, '*and your jaws are too weak*
For anything tougher than suet;
Yet you finished the goose, with the bones and the beak—
Pray, how did you manage to do it?'

'*In my youth,*' *said his father, '*I took to the law,*
And argued each case with my wife;
And the muscular strength, which it gave to my jaw
Has lasted the rest of my life.'

'*You are old,*' *said the youth, '*one would hardly suppose*
That your eye was as steady as ever;
Yet you balanced an eel on the end of your nose—
What made you so awfully clever?'

'*I have answered three questions, and that is enough,*'
*Said his father, '*Don't give yourself airs!*
Do you think I can listen all day to such stuff?
Be off, or I'll kick you down-stairs.'

(LEWIS CARROLL)

Having read both, you will know that the second piece takes less than half the time of the first, and that the tone is brighter with more upward and downward glide of the pitch. It's livelier, nearer to the kind of delivery you use for ordinary conversation. The speech rhythms of the two are different. The first appears to have a succession of light and heavy beats, the second two lights and a heavy; at least that seems to be the basic pattern of the two. If you compare, say, the second lines of each, there is an accented beat in every second syllable in the Keats and every third in the Lewis Carroll, i.e.:

(1) $\smile - / \smile - / \smile - /$: (2) $\smile \smile - / \smile \smile \doteq / \smile \smile .\mathord{\cdot} /$

The first holds the motion back, and, as it were, keeps you in a second gear; the second is lighter and more racy and you prattle along in top gear. Even the same long vowels are longer in the first but the second requires more active consonantal work. This illustrates the two commonest metres used in English poetry. The first is referred to as Iambic metre and the second Anapaestic. The greater the number of heavy beats the slower the motion, which shows more clearly than anything else that *Speech is Action*. Notice the different kind of motion between

'Alone' and pale'ly loit' . . .' and

'And your hair' has become' very white' '

The Iambic is the commonest metre in English poetry and was used by Shakespeare in his unrhymed poetry or blank verse, e.g.:

To be' or not' to be'

But there are variations in its use or it would be very monotonous, just as jazz is more subtle than rock 'n' roll partly because of the greater application of syncopation; the beat is there but is shifted now and then to keep the interest of the ear by the element of surprise.

The sonnet is one of the hardest tests for any speaker, both technically and artistically. It is no wonder that resistance is set up against it by school-children. Few people have the necessary voice control for the speaking of the sonnet, which is spoken too quickly if it takes much less than a minute, i.e. roughly at the rate of a hundred words a minute. Gielgud would probably take it a little faster but he is the verse-speaker *par excellence*: he can be taken as a model but he cannot be emulated.

Compare two sonnets, often used in schools in senior English forms. Both contain exactly the same number of words (109) and almost exactly the same number of syllables, ten to the line, or five Iambic feet. In spite of this equality, the second will take longer to speak than the first. Examine them and you will see that the form is different; the rhyming schemes are not the same. The first, by Shakespeare, is in four quatrains and a rhyming couplet and this is indicated by the rhyme scheme and punctuation. The main idea is stated in the first four lines; elaborated in the second four lines; given a different treatment in the third four lines and brought to an epigrammatic close in the last two. The second, by Wordsworth, might be said to be more contemplative. At least it is dealing with things rather than people and dwells on aesthetic values rather than the human emotions of the first. It has an intensity and conviction of its own but not the same kind of passion as the first.

While content determines interpretation it is the arrangement of words which determines the time for the speaking of each sonnet. Compare the first lines of each. In speaking the Shakespeare one notices there are only two long vowels: 'true', 'minds'. Pedants might protest and insist that the vowel in the second word 'me', is a long vowel and if they insist on accenting the word to force the metre, thus, 'let me,' they will be right but I think the pronoun can be taken for granted and left unaccented in order to provide the cumulative effect necessary for 'marriage of true minds'. Even allowing for three long vowels in the line, there are four long vowels in the first line of the Wordsworth, three of them diphthongs; 'Earth' and 'show', 'more' and 'fair'. Compare the sixth lines of each. In the Shakespeare there is only one long vowel and even that is followed by an unvoiced consonant which reduces its length, 'shaken'. 'Towérs', 'domes', 'theatres' and 'lie', plus the pause used between adjacent nouns gives greater length to the Wordsworth line than is apparent in the Shakespeare. Furthermore the last two lines of the Shakespeare sonnet have an almost pithy quality compared with the feeling of stillness coupled with awed surprise in the last two lines of the Wordsworth.

These two sonnets are worth practising because they present greater difficulty than is to be found in the average dramatic speech. They help to bridge the gap between technique and art; while they cannot be spoken effectively without the application of tone colour they certainly cannot be spoken artistically without the use of imagination. The technique must come first; without it there is no art. Try speaking the first in a few seconds under the minute and the next a few seconds over. There could be a difference of as much as fifteen to twenty seconds.

> 1. *Let me not to the marriage of true minds*
>   *Admit impediments. Love is not love*
>   *Which alters when it alteration finds,*
>   *Or bends with the remover to remove:*
>   *O, no! it is an ever-fixed mark,*
>   *That looks on tempests and is never shaken;*
>   *It is the star to every wandering bark,*
>   *Whose worth's unknown, although his height be taken.*
>   *Love's not Time's fool though rosy lips and cheeks*

Within his bending sickle's compass come;
Love alters not with his brief hours and weeks,
But bears it out even to the edge of doom.
    If this be error and upon me prov'd,
    I never writ, nor no man ever lov'd.

(SHAKESPEARE)

2. *Earth has not anything to show more fair:*
   Dull would he be of soul who could pass by
   A sight so touching in its majesty:
   This city now, doth like a garment, wear
   The beauty of the morning: silent, bare,
   Ships, towers, domes, theatres and temples lie
   Open unto the fields, and to the sky;
   All bright and glittering in the smokeless air.
   Never did sun more beautifully steep
   In his first splendour, valley, rock, or hill;
   Ne'er saw I, never felt, a calm so deep!
   The river glideth at his own sweet will:
   Dear God! the very houses seem asleep;
   And all that mighty heart is lying still!

(WORDSWORTH)

Some readers might find the exercise with the sonnets the most difficult in the book and should not be discouraged if they do not at first get satisfactory results. They would probably be happier with exercises in speech control of a more dramatic nature. There are many good books dealing more comprehensively with the subject. One of the best is Dr Anne McAllister's *A Year's Course in Speech Training*, on page 15 of which is to be found the following:

' "*Extracts for Practice of Intonation.*"
1. (*a*) Don't do that again! (*Speak the words with four different intonations—to express Anger, Fear, Deprecation, Expostulation.*)
   (*b*) This is just what I expected. (*Say the words to express* (*i*) *Delight*, (*ii*) *Anger*, (*iii*) *Despair*.)
   (*c*) So, this is what you tried to tell me about. (*By your intonation express* (*i*) *Delighted Surprise*, (*ii*) *Disappointment*, (*iii*) *Anger*.)

(*d*) *Read with appropriate intonation:*
  (i) What an interesting story!
  (ii) What a sad story!
  (iii) What an amusing story!
  (iv) What a terrible story!
  (v) What an exciting story!

(*e*) Did you know about this before you invited me? (*Deliver the words to suggest (i) Interest, (ii) Reproach, (iii) Anger, (iv) Pleasure, (v) Shame.*)

(*f*) *Read the following in three different ways: Imagining (i) that the lady is setting out on her honeymoon, (ii) that she is on her way to the funeral of one whose death leaves her bereft of home and support, (iii) that she is on her way to prison.*

The road was quite familiar to her, but never had she expected to travel along it under circumstances such as those in which she found herself. Her wildest dreams had failed to picture this. The man by her side seemed to be unmoved by such external circumstances, being intent only on escorting her to her destination. Question after question surged through her mind—What would the future be? How could she face it away from all who had loved her? When would she see her old home again? But suddenly all questioning ceased. The car slowed to a standstill; the door opened; with every nerve quivering, she stepped out and crossed to the gateway.'

The range of voice necessary for the various kinds of drama is obvious but knowing this is an entirely different thing from being able to put it into practice. The approach to contrasting parts such as Lord Goring in Wilde's *An Ideal Husband* and Rosmer in Ibsen's *Rosmersholm* requires a different quality of voice as well as a different attitude of mind.

The possibilities for voice practice with extreme contrasts are inexhaustible. Speeches of a colloquial nature can be eliminated for this purpose. Probably the most artificial speech used in the theatre is that of Restoration comedy and the next poetic drama. Two examples will suffice to illustrate the point:

1. *For men:* (*a*) Vanbrugh's *The Relapse; or Virtue in Danger.* (Act II, scene i), Lord Foppington: from 'That, I must confess, I am not altogether so fond of . . .' to 'Thus, ladies, you see my life is an eternal round O of delights.'

And

(*b*) T. S. Eliot's *Murder in the Cathedral.* The whole of Becket's last speech in Part One, commencing, 'Now is my way clear, now is the meaning plain.'

2. *For women:* (*a*) Congreve's *Way of the World.* (Act IV, scene i) from, Millamant: '. . . . and d'ye hear, I won't be called names after I'm married . . .' to 'I may by degrees dwindle into a wife.'

And

(*b*) Shakespeare's *King Richard III* (Act I, scene ii; first speech). Anne: 'Set down, set down your honourable load . . .'

(*a*) in each case, is excellent for flexibility of voice and
(*b*) good practice for resonance.

You will soon find out whether you are more at home in (*a*) or in (*b*). If, for example, you find more difficulty with (*a*) than with (*b*) find duologues and read both parts for greater continuity, e.g.

1. *For men:* Jack and Algy in the opening of Wilde's *The Importance of being Earnest* and

2. *For women:* Mrs Sullen and Dorinda at the beginning of Act II in Farquhar's *The Beaux' Stratagem.*

If you have practised the foregoing exercises for modulation, rhythm and phrasing—not read them aloud once or even twice but worked at them with frequent repetition and regularity—there should be a considerable improvement in breath control and a general loosening up of the voice. You should now be able to take a much longer selection and 'produce' it with less conscious effort. It is probably too early for you to say definitely what your particular métier is, but you will know whether you respond more easily to comedy or 'drama', whether you take more naturally to blank verse than to colloquial prose or whether you prefer Shaw to Shakespeare. Build up a repertoire of speeches or selections from plays long enough to provide atmosphere and varied enough to demonstrate your talents. Don't hesitate to include an accent or two if you can do this with confidence. Good American accents are rare, in spite of the popularity of authors like Eugene O'Neill, Tennessee Williams and Arthur Miller with amateur groups. Imagine that you are preparing your selections for the purpose of audition; who knows but that you may even fall in for a small part in your local broadcasting or television studio? There is nothing like being prepared! In any case, a producer of your local amateur dramatic society would be impressed with anyone who had gone to so much trouble and could not help noticing your serious approach. He might even cast you in a play on the strength of two or three selections which you had gone to the trouble of learning.

This is not an anthology and half of the book could be taken up with selections from plays, not one of which you would find suitable for public audition. This is where you must exercise your own initiative. Find something fairly complete in itself with a beginning, a middle and an end. Don't depend on the too familiar. Comparisons are odious. If you think that some of the pieces suggested for practice are hackneyed, this was done deliberately until you could find your way around but by this time you have probably done a fair amount of reading and whetted your appetite for material further off the beaten track. We shall find space for one example only, this time for a woman, who could use it for practice. It will be given without comment: you are on your own now!

No Time For Comedy by S. N. Behrman. Act II. Character: Mrs Amanda Smith. Scene: the upstairs living-room of the Smith's New York house.

AMANDA: I don't believe it. You haven't even begun to explore its possibilities. Let me recapitulate it for you. Do you mind? It may restore your perspective on the whole thing.

(GAY *says nothing: he is beyond hope. Suddenly she goes on.*)

A distinguished scientist whose reputation is unimpeachable— Nobel prizewinner in chemistry and all that—has an only son who goes off to fight for the Loyalists in the Spanish War. The boy is killed. He is blown to bits by a German bomb at Guernica. The father finds this fact unbearable. He cannot reconcile himself to it. He simply cannot endure the fact that his beautiful boy—a poet, generous, gifted and sensitive—should be scattered, unrecognizably mangled, in a Spanish suburb . . .

(GAY *sits moodily listening. His brain is settling into a groove of concentration. He begins to feel some resolution impending. She observes this; her beautiful voice goes on hypnotically.*)

Well, he goes on with his work, clings to his work, spends days and nights in his laboratory. One night he falls asleep on his cot for an hour or two, and his son appears to him—his son speaks to him. He wakes up, thinking it a dream, but the communication continues. He begins to investigate psychic phenomena, and he becomes convinced that communication with the dead is possible. He is convinced by the messages he gets from his son. He writes a book and publishes these communications. So that this man, this renowned scientist, the arch-sceptic, this dealer in tested phenomena, who has hitherto regarded all such goings-on as the refuge of the distraught, the stamping-ground for border-cases, marginal hysterics, becomes himself a convert to mysticism, a Prince of the Occult. Because of his scientific eminence, this conversion becomes an international sensation. All over the world the bruised, the grief-stricken, the disinherited, those who, finding life unbearable, idealize death, flock to him for comfort —just as, in another time these same people followed Christ.

(GAY *sits, listening, brooding. He swallows another drink. The cello plays on.*)

To become in one's own lifetime an acknowledged Messiah has its compensations. The scientist delves deeper and deeper into psychic phenomena. The more he delves the more he becomes convinced of their validity. People came to see him from all over the world, just as they came to see Tolstoy. He has a vast correspondence, which it takes a whole staff of secretaries to handle. Gradually he is forced to give up his scientific work altogether. He addresses gigantic meetings.

(*Another pause, and* GAY *takes another drink.*)

Into one of these meetings in the Albert Hall in London a young man wanders. He listens. Suddenly an area clears in his befuddled brain. He remembers. The grey-bearded man on the platform is his father. The past, which has been obscured for him by the horror of his experience in the Spanish War, looms up in his mind. His history begins to take form. He sees it. He remembers where he lived before he enlisted; he wanders out through the streets of London struggling to remember more. Finally, he makes his way to his father's house in St John's Wood. Yes; there it is—his father's house. Yes, he is himself. He has not died in the air-raid. There has been an error in identification. He is his father's son. He has recovered his identity. He goes inside, asks the old servant to see his father. She doesn't remember him, doesn't know him, believing him to be dead. The father has not yet returned from the lecture. She asks him to wait. He sits there, waiting. When suddenly a horrid misgiving strikes him . . . Words spoken by his father in the meeting come back to him. It is borne in on him that his father has a new career, that he is delivering a message to the world, and that this message is based on a single fact—his own death. Will his father want to see him? Dare he be alive? This resurrection from the grave—what will it do but expose to the world another in the long list of the false Messiahs? . . . He looks out of the window and sees the bent old man, his father, his face lined with grief and lit by faith, being helped out of his car. Shall he face him? Shall he go away? He hesitates, his hand on the latch of the door . . . Curtain!

(*A moment,* GAY *sits absorbed and quiet, the highball glass in his hand.*)

CHAPTER SEVEN

Stage lighting

STAGE lighting has become highly specialized in the professional theatre both from the technical and the artistic point of view. To do justice to such an important aspect of the amateur theatre in a book dealing with general principles would be next to impossible. Amateur societies able to operate the lighting plots given in the popular acting editions of West End productions are fortunate indeed to have the experts as well as the equipment. Those seeking the ideal lighting who have the unlimited resources to implement it are advised to study the appropriate sections in *Stage Scenery and Lighting* by Selden and Sellman. Space limits us here to a few brief notes for the beginner working in improvised conditions with inadequate lighting apparatus.

Considered purely in terms of illumination, stage lighting appears at first to be a simple matter. General illumination is not to be despised, though it should be the last item to be considered in any lighting plot. Visibility is as important as audibility. An actor can be heard more easily if his features can be seen clearly, and adequate lighting of the *faces* of the actors is the very first thing to be taken into account when planning the lighting of any production. This must never be sacrificed to style or mood or the creating of atmosphere, whether the play is a comedy or a tragedy or the setting for exterior or interior.

General illumination is provided by units such as footlights, battens, floods and strip-lighting. Specific illumination of actors, acting areas, or objects which require emphasis at a given time is provided by directional or beamed units—the various kinds of spotlights. General illumination is incidental to specific and must therefore be of a lower intensity.

Discriminate lighting can suggest shape and pattern and consequently add greatly to the design of a stage setting. If the illumination is too evenly distributed over the whole of the stage the general picture will be flat and uninteresting. In a realistic interior or an exterior of ordinary daylight, which do not call for great diversity of light and shade, subtle blending of colour can be used to compensate in an otherwise dull picture. Although pools of light and darkness seem to fascinate some producers hard contrasts should be used sparingly and only when they help

113

the dramatic interpretation. Carefully blended areas of light and shade can create the illusion of space and perspective on the stage.

Quantity, position, distribution, balance and colour in the lighting plot of a scene can heighten the emotional content. The psychological effects of lighting were demonstrated in two productions running simultaneously, both musicals of a kind. Both were seen in one day, *Oliver* at the matinée and *Mr Burke*, *M.P.* in the evening. The first, intended as a sentimental comedy, received 'rave' notices and had a long run. It was lighted in warm tones and a variety of colour with plenty of light and shade. The second was a shrewd, brittle political satire which was too strong for at least one hardened critic to sit through. The lighting was in stark white without relief. One wondered what the effect on critics and public would have been if *Oliver* and *Mr Burke*, *M.P.* had exchanged lighting plots. Certainly sympathy for the association of Fagin and the gang of boys led by the Artful Dodger would have been reduced, if not reversed.

The use of colour is largely a matter of taste in spite of the tradition of warmer hues for romantic comedy and sombre tones for tragedy, which may be a fairly safe guide for the uninitiated but is too sweeping a generalization. In fact the same colours could be used for both if quantity and distribution were carefully worked out for each. Usually there is more general illumination for light comedy and greater contrast in light and shadow, provided by specific lighting units, for tragedy. But even in comedy the balance of the lighting must not be sacrificed. The intensity of light should usually be greater downstage than backstage; at the bottom than at the top (there is no point in using specific lighting higher than the level of the actors' faces); centre-stage than towards the wings (except to light an important entrance or to concentrate light at a window in a box-set).

There is no excuse for the crude effects occasionally seen from the use of primary colours (e.g. red, blue and green) in single directional units like spotlights without mixing the colours. Pity the beautiful amateur actress whose lips and cheeks suddenly turn black when she is caught in the deep-blue spot. For the same reason actors should not stray between the cyclorama and its source of light—to say nothing of the phenomenon of human shadows on the sky! Many an otherwise gorgeous costume has been made to appear insipid either because of the wrong **choice** of its colour or lack of foresight regarding the lighting of the scene in which it was to be worn. There is a very wide choice of colour filters for use on the humblest amateur stage. Strand Electric produce no fewer than sixty shades in 'Cinemoid'.

We could take an illustration of a simple lighting plot which could be modified for several plays on an improvised stage with little or no scenery. Most amateurs are acquainted with the school or church hall with the unimaginative 'stage'. It nearly always has an 'apron' jutting out in front of the 'curtain' for speech days and prize distributions or for the vicar to propose a vote of thanks. It probably has a back wall painted in hideous cream (or more hideous brown, in which case you paint it white or provide a sky-cloth) and a couple of sets of traverse curtains.

With a maximum of a dozen spotlights, half of them immediately behind the 'proscenium' and the other half slung in the 'auditorium'; a couple of overhead battens, the first front-stage behind the proscenium and the second a few feet away from the sky-cloth at the back—you might be surprised at the amount of variation which could be provided in the lighting. But it couldn't be done without dimmers. Even so it is as modest a lighting set as any serious amateur group could be expected to possess. You might later be able to add groundrows to light the bottom of your cyclorama for equal distribution of light on your sky, or a couple of floods to light the stage from the sides to kill shadows or to use behind the actors to help with perspective.

Figure 2 is a rough ground plan of the kind of stage referred to. The acting area ensuring visibility from all parts of the hall is indicated by a semi-circle with a dotted line, subdivided again into three smaller acting areas for the various scenes. Even with the limited lighting equipment at our disposal it would be possible to work as many as half a dozen smaller acting areas but this would be hard on anyone working the switchboard and dimmers for the first time. As no scene is likely to be set upstage, none of the spotlights need be directed to the rear of the dotted circle. The acting areas could be lighted in the following manner:

		Spotlights	
Acting Area	*Stage Position*	*F.O.H.*	*Spotbar*
I	Down-centre	7, 9, 10, 12:	2
2	Stage-right	11, 12:	1, 4, 5
3	Stage-left	7, 8	2, 3, 6

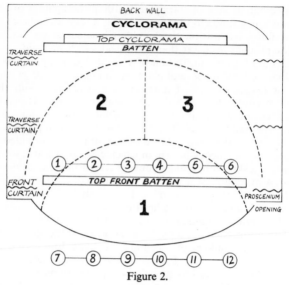

Figure 2.

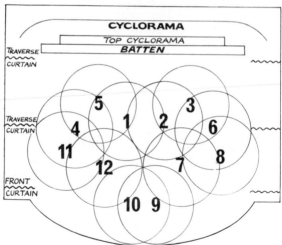

Figure 3.

It will clearly be seen that spotlights could be added or sub-
tracted for any one of the acting areas, which are not necessarily
limited to the space suggested by the dotted lines. Front and
cyclorama battens could be used on dimmers at the discretion
of the producer. Interiors could be set stage right and left, using
the traverse curtains; intimate scenes and duologues might be
played close to the audience in Acting Area 1; ceremonial scenes
could be spread over the whole of the main stage, combining
Acting Areas 2 and 3; the full stage, with as many of the
lighting units as possible, might be kept for exteriors such as
battle scenes, played against the lighted cyclorama.

Figure 3 suggests the possibilities of crossing the beams of spotlights, where possible, at the position of an actor's face, not to
waste the double illumination at the point of the cross above the
heads of the audience. The centre of the beam of each spot,
where it meets the floor of the stage, is indicated by the numbered
circles, but, e.g. No. 8 will reach the *actor's face* at a point
approximately L.C., No. 4 R.C. and No. 2 a little R. of C.
These three have clear filters so that each acting area has at
least one spotlight used solely for the purpose of illuminating an
actor's face, but each is balanced by a spotlight with a coloured
filter, from the opposite direction, e.g. 8 by 6 (pale salmon) and
4 by 1 (pale gold).

Lighting Equipment

The lighting plot illustrated would require a 45 amp. mains
supply at 230/250 volts; 16 circuits, 8 dimmers. All except the
cyclorama are 500 watt circuits, therefore 250/500 or 500/1,000
watt dimmers would be suitable, but 500/1,000 are essential for
the cyclorama.

Spotbar: six 500 watt spots. If you are hiring (or purchasing),
spotlights, you would find the FRESNEL (SOFT EDGE) SPOTS,
Patt. 123, the most effective for directional high-lighting of the
acting area immediately behind the proscenium arch. This unit
can be adjusted to focus on a single actor or flood-light an acting
area. The soft-edge beam merges into that of another Fresnel
spot without cut-off or sharpness. This is a considerable advantage when different colour filters are used with crossed spots,
especially in a small acting area. The following suggestions of
CINEMOID colour filters are made with this in mind. Pale tints
which transmit all the colours of the spectrum—some slightly

less than others—have been chosen deliberately, remembering the scenes in which only a few spotlights are used. Colour for its own sake is useless and mood or atmosphere cannot be created where the actors' faces are not illuminated. The first figure refers to the spot in the plan and the second to the 'Cinemoid' colour filter. Suggested colour filters for spotbar:

1, Pale Gold, 52; 2, Clear, 30; 3, Pale Rose, 54; 4, Clear, 30; 5, Straw, 3; 6, Pale Salmon, 53.

Where economy is the prime factor the JUNIOR SPOT (Patt. 45) could be substituted for Patt. 123. It has the soft-edge beam and is nearly half the price but almost double the weight.

Front-of-house: six 500 watt. PROFILE SPOTS (Patt. 23). The advantage of the 'Mirror Spot' for F.O.H. use is that the shape of the beam can be predetermined. The edge of the beam can be as sharp as desired but the use of diffuser glasses is recommended for softening the edges. 'Spill' from a F.O.H. spot on the proscenium frame or anywhere else in the auditorium distracts the audience's attention from the stage. Four metal diaphragm plates of fixed but different diameters are supplied with this unit but the diameter of circular beams can be varied by using an Iris Diaphragm and a removable Adjustable Mask will provide any shape of four-sided beam. In fact any desired shape can be produced by making a mask of thin metal. The 'Mirror Spot' enables you to shape as well as focus your picture.

Suggested colour filters for F.O.H. spots:

7, Pale Gold, 52; 8, Clear, 30; 9, Gold Tint, 51; 10, Gold Tint, 51; 11, Pale Gold, 52; 12, Pale Salmon, 53.

It is assumed that F.O.H. lighting in an amateur theatre would be nearer to the stage than it is in most professional theatres, where the front of the circle is often the nearest point for this purpose. At the same time they must not be too high and should be at an angle which would compensate for lack of footlights and not too low, to prevent 'spill' on the cyclorama.

It will be seen from the foregoing, that of the dozen spots, three are clear, without colour filters, one of these operating in most scenes to provide a little extra illumination and at the same time blend with the colours from the others. They are directed strategically Right, Left and Centre so that dominating actors in most scenes can take advantage of them.

Cyclorama. Effective sky-lighting in many amateur productions is a matter of trial and error. Most stages are too small to allow for the required distance between the battens, or source of light, and the 'sky'. The actors cannot stand between the two without taking on the colour from the battens and casting a shadow on the 'sky'. There is also the question of equal distribution of light and colour on the surface for the desired effect of infinity. If overhead battens only are used you are left with something approaching sky at the top and nothing better than a lighted wall or cloth at the bottom.

Ground Row battens can be used to balance with top lighting but no provision has been made for these in our lighting plot because we are using an open stage without scenery to camouflage them. However, the front batten could easily be eliminated, thus freeing the circuits for floods, angled, on stands in the wings or behind the back traverse curtains. But if the cyclorama battens can be slung fairly low behind a border and farther away from the cyclorama than shown in the plan, the difference between top and bottom lighting would be negligible. No theoretical lighting plot can be any more than a guide, especially where dimensions and general conditions of the stage can only be guessed at.

Front Batten. This is immediately behind the proscenium and usually between that and the spotbar. In the previous paragraph it was suggested that it might be eliminated. Battens, except for those on the cyclorama, should be used sparingly, if at all, on improvised stages, apart from less imaginative box-set lighting. They are of doubtful value except for general illumination, and can nullify a carefully planned lighting plot, showing up borders and parts of the stage to which you would rather not attract attention. This does not apply to professional stages where the operator has a wide selection of battens higher than on most amateur stages and can ring the changes on a bigger range of circuits.

If you are fortunate enough to own, or wealthy enough to hire, half a dozen JUNIOR FLOODS, Patt. 137, with 150 watt lamps you could use them instead of the batten. They would be a great adjunct to your dozen spots. These could be on two circuits, one with hoods and 52, Pale Gold filters and the other without hoods and 45, Daylight filters.

Footlights. None provided for in the lighting plot and should not be necessary if the F.O.H. spots are carefully positioned and angled. If, however, you have them and insist on their use—like your battens, use sparingly. Don't estimate for them in the light-plot but add them to it for balance after you have tried out the original plot, if you must. They can ruin the effect on the cyclorama or draw the attention of the audience to the actors' knees instead of their faces unless they are carefully positioned, angled and controlled—and they would have to be on dimmers and extra circuits provided for them. Unless you have a particular reason for high-lighting a particular property or piece of scenery, nothing except the faces of the actors requires direct lighting. Scenery, and even costumes if it were possible, are enhanced by reflected light, sufficient of which, for most purposes, comes from the floor.

Switchboard. The use of eight dimmers only has been assumed in the specimen lighting plot but occasionally more than eight circuits might require the use of dimmers. This difficulty can be overcome when necessary by dimming out completely certain of the spots, thus freeing the dimmers for the remaining spots or cyclorama. A detailed plan for the operation of the switchboard should be worked out and interleaved in the script for the exclusive use of the electricians. The various details—switching, dimming and changing of dimmers from one circuit to another—should be rehearsed separately as well as in conjunction with general rehearsals.

CHAPTER EIGHT

Make-up

THE most expert make-up will not play your part for you but the correct make-up will increase your confidence in playing the part. Every actor should learn to make himself up if only for the reason that no expert can ever become as well acquainted with a face as the owner of it. In amateur productions the person brought in specially for make-up usually has too many people to attend to in too short a time and cannot give the same individual attention as can the actor who has learned to make himself up.

How well do you know your face? Which of your ears is higher than the other? Is one side of your face an exact replica of the other in reverse? Carefully examine your features in repose. You may be surprised at the little quirks and oddities you had not previously noticed—if you are a man, of course! Women usually know how to make the most of their faces—with day make-up, but some appear to be unable to carry the same principles into theatrical make-up. Even young women playing juvenile parts have been known to place the colouring on their cheeks too low and too near the front of the soft part of the cheeks, thereby adding ten or fifteen years and transforming a 'straight' part into a 'character' part.

In a 'straight' part grease paint is used for no other purpose than to make the most of yourself—only more so; to counteract the intensity and angles of the artificial light of the theatre and to compensate for the distance between actors and spectators. Grease paint is indispensable with modern theatre lighting. Except for 'character work' theatrical make-up is simply an extension of ordinary make-up for different conditions, using pigments instead of the usual cosmetics. For example, in either case a spot of rouge or carmine is applied to the highest point of the cheek-bone immediately below the extreme outside of the eye and smoothly patted backwards and upwards in the direction of the temple. A little more colour is used for the artificial lighting of the dance-hall than for the daylight of the garden party—and a little more still for the intensity of the theatre spotlight. The proportionate differences are learned only

from experience of the actual circumstances. A little exaggeration
is undoubtedly necessary for the stage but too much of it is to
be deplored. A common fault is to exaggerate one feature at
the expense of the others. The eyes or the mouth may be made
up in great detail with a wealth and variation of colour and the
rest of the face neglected, so that a naturally pretty face is made
to look like a gargoyle. The slight exaggeration for the stage
should be general and the only addition the subtle use of highlights and shadows to offset the flattening effect of the lighting
For this reason alone actors should take an interest in the
lighting, both of colour and intensity, to be used in a particular
production.

Even a 'straight' make-up for one play may be too much or
too little for another. A little more colour may be required to
match up to the costumes and settings of a romantic period
play than for one which demanded nothing more than corduroy
trousers and pullover against a drab kitchen set. The extremes
of farce and tragedy necessitate different tones of colouring.
Leichner, the inventors and largest distributors of grease-paint,
produce a stick (No. $5\frac{1}{2}$, dark ivory), which by tradition is
referred to as 'Hamlet'. 'Sticks' are used for the make-up base,
the first to be applied. No. 5, ivory, is the most commonly used
base. An actor playing the lead in *Roar like a Dove* would find
$5\frac{1}{2}$ too sallow for an open-air extrovert character. He might
choose No. 5 mixed with No. 9 (brownish-red); No. $4\frac{1}{2}$ (reddish-
brown), or Lit. K., which is a combination of 5 and 9. The
decision would depend on his natural colouring and the extent
to which he wanted to modify the complexion towards either a
red or tan shade.

The art of make-up appears in print to be more confusing
than it actually is. Even before the last World War Leichner
listed more than fifty 'sticks', not to mention a further hundred
or so products, including powders, rouges, eye-shadows, liners
and the like. Inevitably the list has been added to for theatrical
purposes alone. Extra products for film and television do not
concern us here. Suffice it to say that for beginners in amateur
acting a make-up kit consisting of a dozen items is quite adequate.
Many competent actors 'make-do' with half a dozen. During
the war, at least one man toured with a revue in which he had
several changes, with his make-up in a match-box, a tin of
talcum powder, a bottle of liquid paraffin for removal—all of

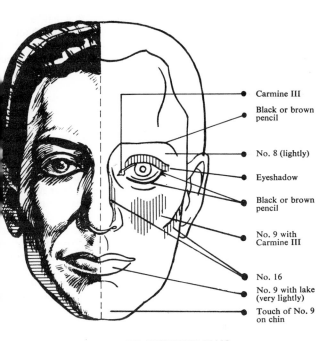

Carmine III

Black or brown
pencil

No. 8 (lightly)

Eyeshadow

Black or brown
pencil

No. 9 with
Carmine III

No. 16
No. 9 with lake
(very lightly)

Touch of No. 9
on chin

LEICHNER JUVENILE MAN

This is a 'straight' make-up; foundation, highlights, and shadows
are used to accentuate your own features. **Foundation:** Use
Greasepaint Standard Stick or Spot-Lite Klear make-up in
tubes. **Shading:** Apply lightly to sides of nose and hollow below
cheekbone, using No. 16, or No. 16 with No. 25 lake. **Highlights:**
Use No. 1½ or No. 5. **Eyes** should be clearly defined with sharp
line along lashes. Shade eyelids with brown—or dark blue, or
dark green for period plays. **Lips:** A little No. 9 and carmine III
is normally sufficient. Be careful not to overdo the lips. **Powder**
with blending powder firmly over the whole make-up, using
rose or neutral shade. Don't forget ears and neck. Apply liquid
make-up to all visible skin. *All shades and numbers given are*
Leichner.

which he carried in a dish-cloth for cleaning. Such parsimony
not recommended.

To begin, practise a 'straight' make-up. Buy half a doze
sticks (or tubes) for base, colouring, highlights and shadow
two or three liners, carmine, powder and cream. Males will b
surprised at the variety which 9 and 5 alone will provide. The
could try the following:

1. Clean the face thoroughly with cold cream and remov
just as thoroughly. Amateurs sometimes make the mistake o
thinking of cold cream as a base.

2. Cover all the visible skin with a light but even applicatio
of No. 5. Don't daub the stick all over your face. A little pressur
of the stick on the cheeks, chin and centre of forehead is sufficien
If you use the same side of the stick throughout you will wea
it wedge-shaped with a nice edge for finer work later on. Usin
the finger tips, spatula fashion, pat in the grease-paint gentl
towards the hair-line of the forehead, eyebrows, eyelashe
behind the ears and towards the nape of the neck. Then, mor
firmly, get an even distribution over the rest of the face, takin
care to fill in all the crevices, e.g. at the base of the nose an
corners of the eyes. You will now appear to be wearing a deatl
mask, which is as it should be. This is the canvas on which yo
will paint, in greater detail, the picture you have obliterated
The analogy could as well be sculpture as painting, you ar
dealing with shape as well as colour.

3. Repeat with No. 9 as for No. 5, but this time not so evenl
Don't make as complete a mask with 9 as you did with 5. Us
more heavily for depressions and more lightly for prominence
Mould it. The merest touch of 9 for flesh tint where the feature
naturally project, the front of the nose from the bridge dowr
immediately above the eyebrows and top front of the chin. Sir
the face where it naturally sinks by making the depression
slightly darker in tone, between the eyelid and eyebrow, betwee
the lower lip and protrusion of the chin, between the outsid
edges of nose and mouth, between the jawbone or behind th
ear to the outside of the 'Adam's Apple', the cleft of the chir
the depression between the nostrils and upper lip; the upper li
slightly darker than the lower (unless you have an 'undersho
jaw when you would reverse the procedure). Your face is nov
beginning to look less lifeless; at least it appears to have mor

shape. You now know the contours of your face. The skin is tighter over bone; the protrusions are bony. The depressions are soft flesh. This is where the hollows come with age, when wrinkles set in over bone, in the forehead and the bridge of the nose, at the outside corners of the eyes. To find out where they *will* come, all you have to do is smile or screw up your face. One of the first rules of make-up is never to paint a depression where it will not come naturally. You can exaggerage or diminish your features by highlighting and shadows but the nearest you can get to a surgical operation is by the use of nose putty or false cheeks (neither recommended). You can shift the hair line with a wig to alter the shape of your face and different shaped beards produce a similar effect. (While you cannot alter the actual shape of your face you can give the appearance of having done so by subtle use of highlights and shadows.) But at the moment we are dealing with a 'straight' make-up.

4. Now draw as thin a line as you can right round the eye as near to the eyelashes as you can, carrying it just a little beyond the outside corner in a slightly upward direction. Use a brown liner for this. Using the same pencil take it lightly round the top of the eyebrow close to the hair. (You can continue this line down the outside edge of the front of the nose, only very lightly for accentuation of the contour.) Use an eyeshadow which matches the natural colouring. Dab a spot on the centre of the eyelid and shade it away gradually towards the corners. Sink the hollow under the eyebrow a little further, carrying the shadow more thinly down the side of the nose inside the line already made. No. 9 will do but when you become more extravagant and more proficient try 8 or 16. Place the tiniest spot of carmine as near to the inside corner of the eye as possible with an orange stick.

5. Get a sharp contour of the lips but do not overcolour. Try a good even coating of 9 with the slightest addition of carmine to the upper lip.

6. Colour the cheeks with 9 in a rough triangle (base upwards), from the point of the cheekbone, patting it away more to the side than to the front. Add a little carmine in a smaller inverted triangle over this.

7. Touch up the highlights and shadows. Add a little shading of No. 8 immediately below the cheekbone between its point and the top of the lobe of the ear. Feel for the hollow. Then

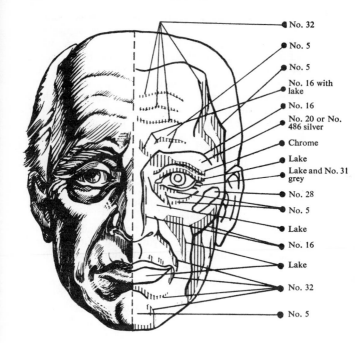

No. 32

No. 5

No. 5

No. 16 with lake

No. 16

No. 20 or No. 486 silver

Chrome

Lake

Lake and No. 31 grey

No. 28

No. 5

Lake

No. 16

Lake

No. 32

No. 5

LEICHNER ELDERLY MAN

In the elderly face wrinkles and facial hollows deepen, muscles and tissues sag, and the skin looks sallow, frequently very delicate. **Foundation:** Use Greasepaint Standard Stick or Spot-Lite Klear make-up in tubes. Select sallow or pastel shades according to type. **Shading:** This should be sharp with a thin line drawn at the deepest part of the shadows. Use mostly Nos. 25 and 32. **Highlights:** To be pronounced, using No. 5. **Eyes:** Define clearly with sharp lines along the lashes using No. 25 or No. 32. For eyeshadow use No. 25 with No. 16 or No. 32. White, dark grey or No. 486 silver cosmetic should be applied to eyelashes. **Lips:** Very careful use of No. 9 with No. 25. **Powder:** Apply rose blending powder firmly over make-up, brush off surplus. **Hair:** White or grey hair powder, or No. 486 silver cosmetic. Remember to make-up hands and neck. *All shades and numbers given are* Leichner.

highlight it with No. 5 round the edge of the cheekbone. But don't overdo either for a 'straight' make-up. You could mix, almost imperceptibly, the tiniest spot of lake with 8, especially for just below the lower lip, the crevices of the chin and upper lip. You could highlight with No. 5 the upper edge of the cheekbone, the point of the jawbone and the protruding ridges of the upper lip.

Examine your make-up carefully before you apply blending powder. It is assumed that you have a good light directed on to your face and not into the mirror, without shadows. The nearest you can get to an idea of how the audience sees you is to half close your eyes and look at your reflection through your eyelashes. See that your ears are not left highlighted with No. 5. Tone them down with No. 9 if they are. Get a good firm powder puff, not a fluffy one. Don't rub the powder on and don't try to be too economical. Press the puff firmly into the powder and then press the powder firmly into your face until all the make-up is covered. You will now look as you did after the application of the base of 5. Now take a soft brush and get rid of as much of the powder as you can, especially from eyebrows, eyelashes, hairline, and crevices of the face. The tones of the grease-paint will have blended one into another and your make-up will have an attractive matt finish for standing up to the bright lights of the stage. You may have to touch up with powder between the acts. Do it carefully and see you get the same consistency.

It is more important than ever to remember that make-up can be little more than an aid to a 'character' part, which depends primarily on acting. If the voice and body cannot be adapted or modified for the character no amount of make-up will create the desired illusion.

When you have acquired a degree of mastery with a straight make-up, you can experiment with a character make-up. You can, in fact, age yourself considerably simply by repeating what you have already done, except that you will substitute different coloured sticks and liners and further accentuate highlights and shadows. By using a mixture of lake and grey for the depressions and No. 20 (or No. 1) for the highlights and eliminating the brighter tones, especially carmine, you have the beginnings of a rather ferocious old man. Take out the fullness as well as the colour of the lips, giving a downward droop to the mouth at the corners. Screw up your face and draw in the wrinkles lightly with a pencil—but only as a guide for shading and highlighting these. Shadows and highlights are complementary; one cannot exist without the other. Don't think in terms of 'lines' or your face will look like a road map under the stage lighting. Lining is one of the worst faults of make-up on the amateur stage, where 'crows' feet' appear to be the most popular form! Shade in the hollows of the cheeks with lake and grey, also the hollow of the eyebrow through to the side of the nose-bridge down to a point slightly below the inside centre of the eye.

It is not possible to give any more than a rough guide to a character make-up through the medium of print. You might find in practice that lake and grey gives too stark an effect and that you have a preference for using No. 16. You must experiment. For instance, chrome can provide the parchment effect which occasionally comes to the skin with age, especially over bone, as in the temples. Remember that wrinkles are not inevitable with age and that some old people have beautifully clear complexions. You could have an elderly woman with silver hair and a face like Dresden china. Be careful not to alter the character of a gentle old man into that of an evil old roué with sunken eyes and beak nose, by piling on the lake!

For further practice, invest in a set of Leichner Make-up Charts, examples of which are given. They are only sixpence each and give a wealth of valuable information.

Wigs: Never use one unless it is imperative. If you have to, see that it is a good one and give it the same careful treatment you would your own hair—on and off your head. See that it is straight and that the hair-line is in the correct position. There is usually a small tab fitted to the front of each ear, to help you to find the right position and pull it tight over your scalp. Women can study illustrations of period hair-styles to find out whether their own hair can be dressed in the correct manner before submitting themselves to wearing a wig. Good ones are very expensive even to hire. They are, of course, indispensable for certain parts, e.g. male characters in Restoration plays.

Beards and moustaches: Shapes and sizes of these depend on period and nationality. In *A Dictionary of English Costume, 900–1900*, Cunnington and Beard (!) tell us that in the hundred years from the mid-sixteenth to the mid-seventeenth centuries there were over fifty named cuts of beard in fashion and describe

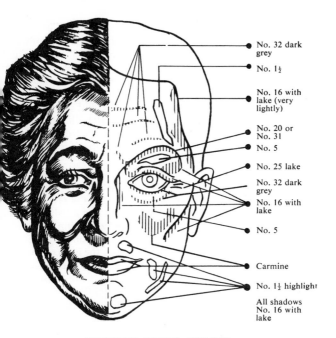

No. 32 dark grey

No. 1½

No. 16 with lake (very lightly)

No. 20 or No. 31

No. 5

No. 25 lake

No. 32 dark grey

No. 16 with lake

No. 5

Carmine

No. 1½ highlight

All shadows No. 16 with lake

LEICHNER JOVIAL WOMAN

A pleasant elderly face with softly rounded folds and strongly marked highlights and shadows. **Foundation:** Use Greasepaint Standard Stick or Spot-Lite Klear make-up in tubes. Select shades from catologue. **Shading:** Place soft pools of shading as indicated, accentuated by sharp lines of lake or dark grey at deepest part. Use No. 25 lake with No. 16. **Highlights:** Should be freely applied using No. 1½ or No. 5. **Eyes:** Draw sharp lines along lashes using No. 32 dark grey. For eyeshadow use No. 16 with lake, or mauve, purple or dark blue. No. 486 silver cosmetic on eyebrows. **Lips:** Apply carmine III lightly keeping the outline soft—don't overdo it. **Powder** with rose blending powder firmly over make-up, brush off surplus. **Hair:** A touch of No. 486 silver cosmetic on hair is very effective—also Grey or white hair powder. Apply liquid make-up to neck, arms, and hands. *All shades and numbers given are* **Leichner.**

a dozen of these in detail with illustrations of quite a numbe
throughout the period covered in the book.

Within recent years good quality ready-made beards an
moustaches with pliable gauze bases for easy fixing with spir
gum have been on the market. The actor who takes a pride i
his craft will derive more satisfaction from making his own fror
crêpe hair, which can be bought by the yard. Amateurs hav
been known to use it as it comes from the makers, which is
mistake. It is packed tightly round string and crinkled, whic
gives it a curly or waved effect when unpacked. The string shoul
be removed, and the crêpe hair slightly dampened and wrappe
firmly around a solid object such as a chair-back for straighter
ing, so that it is ready for use when dry.

Apply spirit gum, with a brush, to that part of the face t
which the hair is to be fixed. Let it get 'tacky'. Observe how th
hair grows naturally, downwards. Don't put the crêpe hair fla
on the face. Spread the ends out an inch and a half or so an
cut a straight edge; fix it immediately *under* the chin and cut ju
under the desired length of the beard. Repeat on the lower *fron*
of the chin. Then *build* your beard. Spread the ends of the crêp
hair a little wider than the first time and fix another piece unde
the chin behind the first and a fourth piece *above* the second o
the front of the chin; these two pieces slightly longer than th
first two. Repeat until you reach the positions below the bottor
lip and the angle of chin and neck. Press the hair to the skin a
the front and below the chin with a stretched towel. When firm
cut and trim the beard to the shape and size required.

For a moustache, start at the bottom of the upper lip, usin
narrower pieces of hair towards below the nose and thinnin
out towards the top, then trim. Likewise for side-whisker
fixing pieces of hair one above the other towards the hair-lin
near the top of the ear.

Hair on the face is usually a little lighter in shade than that o
the scalp, so if you have dark hair give yourself a mid-brow
beard. Jet-black beards, moustaches and side-whiskers are rathe
rare. Facial hairs are generally of different tones. If slight variant
of the same colour are used for alternate layers of a beard an
combed for mixing, it will look more natural.

Don't forget that the hands can be almost as expressive as th
face and the attention of the audience is constantly being draw
to them. They too, require make-up, especially in characte

parts. If you are a sedentary worker playing a horny-handed son of the soil your hands could belie the efforts you had made on your face unless you gave them the same attention. Or if you are a manual or outdoor worker playing a lily-livered duke, when you lift that glass of champagne or expensive cigarette-holder, the contrast between hand and face could kill the effect you had carefully sought after, unless the hand toned in with the face. You can use grease-paint on your hands but liquid make-up is more satisfactory for straight parts, especially if you have to put your hands in your pockets or run your hands through the heroine's hair.

Make-up of some kind should be applied to all exposed flesh. A woman in evening dress who made up her face and neglected her chest and back would look either like a touched-up corpse or a 'shining' example of how not to appear on the stage. But women, at least, don't often have to be told about such things.

CHAPTER NINE

Costume

THE actor must carry the costume, not the costume the actor. A good actor can persuade his audience into believing that an old sheet is a genuine toga; a poor actor cannot convince his audience that the most expensive costume is any other than an old rag. It is a waste of money to provide elaborate costumes if the actors are incapable of wearing them. There is more in wearing clothes than good physique. A good actor with indifferent physical attributes can have a better carriage than his less gifted but more handsome colleagues. Moreover, there is a close association between movement and costume, particularly so in period or historical plays.

The way an actress walks in classical, medieval, Restoration or Victorian roles will vary according to the restriction imposed or the freedom allowed by the costume she wears. A mincing Greek or striding Edwardian woman would, to say the least, be out of character. The gym mistress who is cast as Elizabeth Barrett has to remember that she is not wearing a 'gym' tunic. An actress who is incapable of adapting her carriage, gesture and general movement to characters as varied as Antigone, St Joan, Millamant and Lady Precious Stream will not expect to be considered for a wide range of parts. There are indeed few professional actresses capable of such versatility.

Costume is not a disguise but an auxiliary to characterization and a sense of period. A labourer limited to the use of a pick and shovel would not be expected suddenly to display the lightness of touch required for the rapier, any more than an office clerk whose only means of locomotion had been the bus and the escalator would appear at home in a ploughed field for the first time. Neither could disguise the facts merely by dressing up as a courtier or a farm labourer. A complete reorientation of muscular balance would also be necessary. The actor has to adapt his body to the costume and this requires both mental and physical training.

Slavish adherence to accuracy in historical costume can be as much of a hindrance as a help in theatrical production. It was not considered of importance until fairly recently. Actors or

Elizabethan and Jacobean times were content with contemporary costuming of Shakespeare's plays, as was the custom until the nineteenth century, with notable exceptions such as Greek and Roman plays. The best modern producers respect historic detail only insofar as they are in keeping with the general plan of production; the décor, the colour, the lighting and the prevailing mood of the play. Artistic unity must not be sacrificed to historical realism. At the same time, a knowledge of the history of costume is just as vital as aesthetic appreciation, if only to guide the producer in deciding how far dramatic licence can be carried. Confusion between the sixteenth-century farthingale and the nineteenth-century crinoline would be unpardonable.

Compromise with regard to *making* costumes and the materials used, depends largely on the period of the play. The Greeks 'draped' their figures in woollens and linen, with great simplicity in full and flowing lines. The English nobility of the Restoration embellished their bodies, fussily and extravagantly with footling ornamentation, in lace, satins and velvet, richly lined and heavily embroidered. Of the two, the Greek is easier to imitate for stage purposes. Cheesecloth, which is the cheapest material available, hangs well if it is full enough to allow for pleating and gathering: only a highly experienced wardrobe mistress could provide the cut necessary for reproduction of the dress of a courtier of Charles II. Rough imitations of costumes for Biblical or Anglo-Saxon periods are often acceptable but he would be a foolhardy producer who left the provision of a houppelande of the late fourteenth or early fifteenth centuries to an amateur seamstress. As rich a garment as this would have to be hired to be effective. The most elegant period in the history of British costume was probably during the reign of Charles I and any attempt to dress plays of this time should be left to the best professional theatrical costumiers.

A study of the history of costume is rewarding for its own sake. It throws interesting highlights on the people and reflects the nature of the times.

A knowledge of period costume is necessary if only for checking items hired from theatrical costumiers. A wardrobe mistress who gives the impression of knowing what she wants when ordering will get better service than one who is content with filling in the official measurement forms sent by the firm. One who waits until a fortnight before the production must accept what the firm can offer from existing stocks at short notice, in fit, cut, material and colour. Consultation with the producer should be held in the early stages of production about décor, lighting, colour, grouping, mood and general interpretation, in order that the wardrobe mistress can take her share of responsibility for her contribution to the visual effect, which is an essential part of the production. Measurements should be checked and rechecked, bearing in mind the mobility of the character and the under-garments to be worn with the costume. Theatrical costumiers respect the wardrobe mistress who gives care and attention to detail and will go out of their way to give satisfaction, even to hiring from other firms if given plenty of notice of requirements.

Accessories are as important as the main garments. Amateur actors have a habit of seeming to appear half-naked even though they are covered from neck to ankle in expensive hired costumes. They go on to the stage, happily, in the bare essentials provided by the theatrical costumiers—and that's that! But the costume is only the groundwork. Having dressed their bodies in the costume they must then dress the costume. Obviously too much is too much, but a Victorian papa without a watch-chain and fob, his daughter without her fan or his housekeeper without her girdle for keys, are not ready for a fancy-dress ball—let alone a dramatic production. Hats, shoes, gloves, parasols, handkerchiefs, scarves, shawls, beads, buckles, brooches, hair ornaments and appropriate jewellery with hand properties carefully chosen, can enhance the costume a hundred-fold. It is worth noting that a string of large, coloured wooden beads can be more effective theatrically than an expensive necklace of real pearls.

Making the most of the costume has already been mentioned but there are subtleties of stance and gesture in association with costume which are too often ignored. These are, of course, the producer's responsibility. Nothing is more unsightly, for example, than to see an actor adopting a pose he might habitually use in a pair of loose old flannel trousers, when he is wearing skin-tight hose on the stage. The knees are bent, the stomach sags and the shoulders droop. The actor in hose should practice different stances, e.g. when facing the audience, with hands on hips (closed fist, not fingers or thumbs forward—it makes all the difference!) and legs astride. When standing sideways to the audience he could practise standing with his upstage foot forward, knee slightly bent, the downstage knee flexed well back, the downstage hand (fist) on hip, the upstage elbow resting on the hip with the hand relaxed to the side-front of the abdomen. And do see that those 'tights' are tight! Brace them, to avoid those too common unsightly wrinkles, by twisting halfpennies in the top for buttons. Failing braces, twist a coin into the top at each side of the waist for security. If they have seams, see that they are straight.

A costume is always displayed to better advantage by standing with the upstage foot forward—instage—apart from the fact that the upstage foot in that position acts as a lever to swing you round in the direction of the audience if you have to speak a line to another character upstage of you. The same principle applies to kneeling on the stage. Characters are rarely asked to kneel on both knees, except for, say, total abjection. For respect or obeisance, or the curtsey, only one knee is lowered to the ground. Consider the pictorial effect alone of an actress in a rich and full period costume with train, kneeling to a character upstage of her—on her upstage knee! The folds of the dress between the downstage calf and the upstage knee are lost to the audience; the train is more or less out of sight, following a line from her backstage foot to the upstage wing. The costume is wasted and the picture aesthetically unsatisfying. Now consider, from the audience's viewpoint, the effect with the actress on her downstage knee. Assume that she is stretching her upstage hand, shoulder high, in a gesture towards the character upstage of her. Examine the line of the drape from, say, her right fingers to her left toes. Every fold of the dress is visible to the audience; it flows rhythmically down from the forearm, through the upstage knee and the downstage foot and beyond to the spread train and seemingly, on into the auditorium at a point stage-left. The costume has added pattern to the play and personality to the actress. It was an investment which has paid dividends.

Period costume usually requires broader, and often higher gesture than the pernickety jabs and thrusts which go with contemporary dress. A fairly safe rule, so long as it is not over-done, in classical and certain Shakespearean productions, is to keep the basic gestures shoulder high in rhythmical curves outwards from the lower chest. The Greeks—and even the English of the Elizabethan era—were as uninhibited as present-day Latin continentals. As late as the Georgians the English still had style. A rough guide, in the eighteenth-century play, is to keep the hands about waist high. Snuff-boxes, lorgnettes, fans and general appurtenances of the period will help in this. If you have no easily accessible pockets you must do something with your hands. Make them act for you! When you sit down in your eighteenth-century velvet or satin breeches, silk stockings and buckled shoes—don't be afraid to 'show a leg'. Elegant abandon was the order of the day for the gallants. You need not always sit back sternly in the angle of the chair like a Victorian martinet. You can 'loll' nearer the front of the seat, your shoulder blades supported by the high back of the eighteenth-century chair with both legs stretched out; or with one stretched and the other bent with heel raised just under the chair, knees splayed, toes turned out, one hand on hip, the other playing with a quizzing glass.

If you are an actress wearing a nineteenth-century bustle you will forget your golf-stance. Nor will you sit down in the manner of a modern kennel-girl or schoolgirl hockey champion. Outdoor women and 'tweedy' types often stand straddle-legged in front of a chair, drop their heads between their knees and throw their posteriors into the air before dropping them heavily from a great height into the chair, after which they throw their heads up and back with a guffaw, legs stretched, knees wide, with only their heels touching the floor—as good as the next man! No, you will walk demurely but with with assured deportment to the chair and inconspicuously feel for the edge of the seat with the back of your leg, gently raise the bustle with your finger tips, and lower your trunk slowly and perpendicularly on to the chair—and sit as though there was still air between it and you. When you walk across the stage you will hold your head as though your hair was being held by someone in the 'flies', just allowing your feet to touch the ground.

An actress playing medieval or classical parts can take slightly longer but none the less graceful strides when heavily draped, or when wearing a costume of especially heavy material. As she walks the knee should be in advance of the toe—the opposite of the walk in a modern evening dress when the toe is in advance of the knee—so that the knee and thigh take the weight of the material or drapery. In a crinoline she will take smaller steps so that propulsion is imperceptible as a walk, as though she were on wheels, so that the toes never protrude under the dress.

Probably more books have been written on costume than on any other single aspect of the theatre. There are certainly too many to give even a suggestion of the quantity and variety in a book attempting to cover the amateur theatre generally. The series by Iris Brooke would be an excellent introduction to the subject. If one is tempted to recommend a single volume for the serious beginner, Lucy Barton's *Historic Costume for the Stage* is probably as comprehensive as any. In approximately 600 pages it covers costume in great detail and in chronological order from 4000 B.C. (Egyptian) to the early twentieth century; is well illustrated and offers practical suggestions for the making of the costumes.

CHAPTER TEN

Effects, properties and incidentals

'EFFECTS' covers a wide range of visual and aural devices demanding the imaginative use of lighting, music and other sounds. The *effects man* can ruin a scene or unintentionally cause laughter in the auditorium. Take a very simple example: Two characters, a man and a woman, have an angry scene which is interrupted by the approach of a third character off-stage left. The *effects man* is given a cue by the woman for approaching feet or the sound of a door opening, which in turn is the cue for the man to look or indicate off-stage left and say, 'Hush! Someone's coming.' The *effects man* is on the wrong side of the stage and shuffles his feet or bangs a door *off-stage right*! The audience laughs at the incongruity; the entrance of the third character and the ensuing scene are ruined.

At a performance of *Blithe Spirit* in an Irish drama festival, the producer wanted a green 'following' spot on Elvira. Either it was a last-minute decision or the effect was under-rehearsed. Probably the man working the spot was inexperienced or Elvira was awkward! Throughout the performance the spot was, disconcertingly, on everyone and everything—except Elvira. Interest in the play became secondary to speculation as to whether she would be caught in the spot on her next entrance and bets were laid on the probability. Excitement ran high and it wasn't until the very end of her last entrance that the man on the spot-light succeeded in training the spot on Elvira. The cry '*Got her!*' rang through the auditorium, followed by loud and prolonged applause.

Not all audiences are as sporting as this Irish one.

Stage-managers do not always appreciate that *Noises-off*, or off-stage effects require, if anything, more preparation and rehearsal than on-stage effects. That which can be heard but not seen lacks the same credibility for the audience as that which, as it were, can be both seen and heard. Noises-off should, generally, be louder than noises-on; without, of course, the element of shock or spoiling of theatrical illusion. They should be definite and 'dead on cue' so that they do not sound accidental if they are mechanical, or like back-stage interruptions if they are human. (Incidentally, crowds off-stage should always be given specific dialogue even though the audience cannot recognize the words. There is far too much 'Rhubarb, rhubarb, rhubarb' passed off for crowd effects on the amateur stage by super-numeraries dragged in too late for production. Individual speeches or off-stage cries should be practised for pitch and volume. The actor should learn to 'throw' his voice for such occasions.)

Most mechanical noises can be reproduced mechanically or electrically nowadays. It should be remembered that the *engine* of a modern car can rarely be heard from a distance. Tyres on gravel, the squeak of brakes or the opening and closing of a car door (not the sound of a prison gate) are the best indications of an approaching vehicle. When the telephone bell rings be sure that the sound and appearance of the instrument match; both have changed over the years.

Nearly all sound effects can be hired. STRAND ELECTRIC list among other things for hire, the following:

> *Electrical:* Single door or double telephone bell sets, buzzer-sets, door-chimes, smoke-box, flash-box, bomb-tanks.
> *Hand-operated:* Rain-box, wind, thunder-sheet.

However, some amateur societies attract men of imagination and powers of invention who enjoy providing effects of their own making.

Some of the time-honoured, hand-operated methods of producing effects sound more like the real thing than do record-ings of the actual sounds. They are often safer and easier to bring in on cue. Recordings on tape or gramophone are often difficult for split-second timing of cues even when they are pre-set, though they obviously cannot be done without for music cues. But for anything as instantaneous as *thunder* nothing is more effective than the old-fashioned thunder-sheet, which is nothing more than a sheet of metal hung by a rope in the wings to be shaken and controlled on cue. Different kinds of thunder can be produced by a large sheet of heavy metal for a threatening rumble, or a small piece of light photographic ferrotype sheeting for a startling crackle.

A *wind machine* can be made out of a small barrel (not too broad in the beam) with top and bottom, an old car starting handle and a box slightly longer than the barrel, with the bottom and one of the longer sides removed. Insert the car handle through the centre of the top and bottom of the barrel so that the barrel will turn with the handle. Remove some of the slats of the barrel so that you have a slat and a space alternating. Stand the box on its remaining long side, cut a groove in the top centre of each of the short sides. Fit the barrel between these with the car handle resting in the grooves. Lay a piece of canvas over the barrel, nailing the ends of the canvas, fairly tightly, to the bottom—or long side of the box. By revolving the handle the effect of wind is produced. The volume of noise, from a breeze to a hurricane, is controlled by the speed at which you revolve the handle.

For *rain*, peas or rice rolled on a drum or a tin tray can sound quite realistic. The playing of a pair of coconut shells one against the other for *horses' hooves* on cobble-stones is well enough known.

A combination of *sea-sounds*, *storm* and *wind* can be effected by a discreet 'orchestration' of wind machine, peas or rice on tray or drum, plus an electric fan, out of sight, blowing on a curtain or window-blind—if you have the stage-staff.

Bangs, *crashes* or even *shots*, can be simulated by a slat or piece of wood, with one end held in the hand and the other end with the foot acting as a hinge to the timber and the floor. The hand is released and the foot pressed simultaneously so that the timber hits the floor sharply. The quality of the sound is modified by the thickness and length of the timber, the hollowness or solidity of the floor and the force with which both meet.

Breaking glass is done with—believe it or not—broken glass! Have a bucket half-full of broken glass and tip it sharply into another, empty, bucket. An actor can produce the illusion of breaking a window from outside, in full view of the audience, simply by putting the fist of one hand through an imaginary pane and dropping a brick into a bucket of broken glass behind the window, with the other hand.

My own opinion is that noises-off can nullify illusion more than they assist it and should be used sparingly. A good actor can suggest by miming, what he is supposed to hear off-stage. Sound effects often unnerve the actor and get between him and his audience to the detriment of interpretation. The storm in *King Lear* is provided through the medium of Shakespeare's word-pictures. No thunder-sheet can be as expressive as:

> 'Blow, winds, and crack your cheeks! rage! blow!
> You cataracts and hurricanoes, spout
> Till you have drench'd our steeples, drown'd the cocks!'

or,

> 'Rumble thy bellyful! Spit, fire! spout, rain!'

and it would be nothing short of sacrilege to obscure such words with any sound effect. Minimize the mechanics and keep your production as human as possible. At least one producer had artistry enough to present the storm scene in *Lear* without having to resort to mechanical sound effects. He had the 'Fool' clinging to Lear like a leech and whining like the wind into his chest, so that the sound was always under and never interfered with Lear's lines. I doubt whether more than a few discerning members of the audience, and even then only those in the front row, knew how the effect of the wind was produced. This producer believes in leaving as much of the interpretation as possible to the actors—to whom the stage belongs.

Visual or *optical* effects range from the childishly simple to the extremely difficult, the latter often beyond the resources of many amateur dramatic societies. In a production of *Journey's End*, the 'Very' lights in the distance were done simply by punching a curved line of small holes in the small piece of sky-cloth at the entrance to the dug-out, along which the stage-manager drew a lighted torch on cue.

To provide falling *snow* outside a normal-sized window, all that is necessary is to hang a feather bolster above the window, make a slit along the bottom and control the fall of the feathers. For snow in an exterior scene torn paper can be sprinkled from above but this is cumbersome and untidy. Where a cyclorama or sky-cloth is available a projection lantern can be hired for the optical effect.

Smoke, *fog*, *mist* or *clouds* can be produced actually by a smoke-box, if you can control the density or direction and shape and avoid choking your actors. A gauze dropped in front of the scene is more comfortable but it will not provide shape or moving clouds. This would require the optical effect from a projection lantern on the cyclorama.

Electrical or clockwork optical effects for fleecy clouds, storm clouds, rain, snow, waterfall or running water, flames, sea wave, water ripple and dissolving colour, may be hired from lighting firms.

The following sound effects records are available from H.M.V. They may be re-recorded for private purposes or by amateur film societies, and also may be used without licence fee for public performances by private individuals and by amateur dramatic societies.

Air Raid on London. Warning; Plane approaches; Gunfire; Bombs falling; Fire engines; Gunfire; Shell bursts; All Clear. **Air Raid Effects.** Bombs falling; A.A. fire, planes and bombs falling; A.A. fire, wardens' feet and explosion (7FX1). **Car Effects.** Revving and departure; Approach and pass; Arrival; Departure; Approach and pass; Reverse; Horns; Sirens; Door, starter, ticking over; Door, starter and depart; Approach and skid; Crash (7FX2). **Church Bells.** Call to service; Call changes—suitable for weddings (7FX3). **Dogs.** House dogs barking; Alsatians barking and howling; Small dogs barking, yelping, barking at distance; Terriers barking at intruder (7FX4). **Horses.** Horses: galloping on turf, trotting on gravel; Single horse on gravel: walking; trotting; cantering; galloping; Horse and carriage arriving and departing (7FX5). **Sea Effects.** Wash on shingle; Seagulls (7FX6). **Rain.** Heavy. **Ships.** Sirens and hooters (7FX7). **Thunderstorm.** Approaching and receding; Overhead (7FX8). **Trains.** Express: passing with whistle; passing; crash. Local passenger: arriving, door slam, guard's whistle, depart. Express journey complete (7FX9). **Wind.** Gale force; High wind; Hurricane and eerie wind (7FX10). **Birds.** Dawn chorus; Nightingale; Owls, barn and screech (7FX11). **Street Noises.** General traffic noises. **Applause.** Excited applause outdoor, indoor; Applause, Outdoor; Concert applause (7FX12). **Aeroplanes.** Air liner: passing overhead; Engine noise, interior; Nose dive, crash and fire. Jets: Warming up and taking off; Landing and taxiing; Flying on full boost (7FX13). **Demolition.** Falling debris, demolition, explosion; With water and fire. Glass crashes and hammering. Glass crashes, workmen hammering (7FX14). **Space Ships.** Take off; Rising and falling; Continuous vibration; Low hum with tick; Low hum with bursts of air. **Various Ghost Effects** (7FX15). (Fifteen 7 in., 5s. 3d. plus 1s. 8½d. P.T. each.)

'Properties' usually refers to all articles used on the stage other than costumes, scenery and lighting. Some producers exclude larger units of furniture and confine the 'props' list to smaller items such as those which are directly concerned with the action of the play; movable articles, food and eating utensils, telephones, firearms, writing materials, etc. Hand properties or personal 'props' produced on cue by the actors—flowers, letters, telegrams, sewing materials, cigars and cigarettes or anything referred to in the script from books to budgerigars, are the responsibility of the property master. He collects all such articles at the end of each performance and checks each one before the rise of the curtain on the next. The property master must see that actors have personal properties on their persons before they make their entrances. He will have a 'props' table at the side of the stage, to which is attached a list of vital properties, numbered for reference and checking.

The property master has to be a craftsman as well as something of a magician. For example, if he is asked to provide a 'trick' table for the banquet scene in *The Tempest* (Act III, Scene iii) which has to be worked by the actors, they must have absolute confidence in him. He makes a table with a top which will swivel round in its frame, bottom up, at a touch. It can be done with the ball and socket type of door catch fixed to the centre of the short edges of table-top and frame and camouflaged some distance down the front and sides. But that is the easiest part of the 'prop'. The table-top must be laid with the 'banquet': goblets, dishes, fruit and apparently luscious food—all of which has to 'vanish' on cue. Obviously, china, metal and real food cannot be used. All articles must be light-weight and glued to the table-top so that they are suspended from it when it revolves and are hidden by the camouflaged sides of the table. Nor must any article be higher than half the width of the table-top or they will 'jam' the operation. Dishes, goblets and food can be made from cardboard, or better still, for solidity or three-dimensional effect, from *papier mâché* and painted in rich colours. The heavier articles can be dressed on the central line of the table so that a slight pressure by an actor on cue 'thunder and lightning', will revolve the top. The stage directions are:

'*Enter Prospero above, invisible. Enter several strange Shapes, bringing in a banquet: they dance about it with gentle actions of salutation; and, inviting the King, &c., to eat, they depart.*'

Thirty lines or so later, Alonso says,

> 'I will stand to, and feed,
>   Although my last: no matter, since I feel
>   The best is past. Brother, my lord the duke,
>   Stand to, and do as we.'

which is followed by another stage direction:

> '*Thunder and lightning. Enter Ariel, like a harpy; claps
> his wings upon the table; and, with a quaint device, the
> banquet vanishes.*'

On 'I will stand to . . .' Alonso comes down in front of the
table, facing upstage, and on 'Brother, my lord the duke!
Stand to . . .', the rest complete a circle round the table as if to
eat. On 'Thunder and lightning' Alonso raises his arms in alarm
as if to shield his eyes and in doing so, spreads his cloak, hiding
the table from the audience. At the same moment, Sebastian or
another actor shielded from the audience by Alonso's cloak,
clutches the table as it were for support, and by pressure of the
thumb or finger revolves the table-top, causing the 'banquet'
to vanish, leaving the actors free to move on Ariel's speech.

It will readily be seen that to give instructions for making
individual properties used in innumerable plays, would require
a whole book. Consider one category alone; musical instruments.
You require a flageolet for J. B. Fagan's *And So to Bed*, or a
cittern for Ben Jonson's *The Alchemist*. You will find illustrations
of both, with dozens of other line drawings of 'props' in *Stage
Properties* by Heather Conway. The book gives descriptions of all
kinds of out of the way articles with instructions for making
and assembling them. Among other things, it gives the preparation and uses of *papiér mâché* in detail.

Music in the theatre requires the attention of the specialist,
especially if it is incorporated in the play. In period plays even
introductory or interval music should be chosen with care. The
insensitive choice of incidental music can ruin the mood which
the producer and actors have been at pains to create. A good
music adviser can provide a fair imitation of the sound of a
period instrument no longer procurable. This is done in the
wings while the actor mimes playing the 'dummy' on the stage.

Gramophone and tape-recorder should be used with discrimination. Too much volume is the commonest offence in the amateur theatre. There is no need to make the place sound like a fair-ground. The merest suggestion of music will produce the desired effect.

There is usually more than one setting to the songs in Shakespeare's plays and the producer is advised to hear as many as possible before deciding which is the most suitable for his particular interpretation. Few amateur producers are accomplished musicians. Neither have they the time for reading esoteric and expensive books on music for the stage, which can amount to exhaustive research. But there are some inexpensive little books which offer practical suggestions, even giving record serial numbers for period plays, dances and songs. The series, *Playing Period Plays*, by Lyn Oxenford, in four parts, $1.00 each, has helpful sections on the subject.

CHAPTER ELEVEN

Copyrights; royalties; performing rights

I T should be remembered that reproduction of music from gramophone records and sound or television programmes for public performance is subject to performing rights. Permission of the owners of the copyright must be sought for tape-recordings of copyright material. Even if you use recordings of your own efforts on the piano you should find out whether the score is subject to copyright.

Remember also that many plays are the property of the author and that he or his agent both have people with their interests at heart in the most remote places. The author may be dependent for his livelihood on the royalties he receives from amateur performances of his plays. Application for permission to perform must be made and, usually, the fee paid in advance.

Generally, the copyright expires fifty years after the death of the author, but this does not cover all translations, of, e.g. Ibsen, who died in 1906. Make sure that the translator has no claim before you decide to perform a certain play because you think there is no fee.

You must also conform to the regulations and requirements of your local authority. Find out whether your premises are satisfactory to the police and the fire brigade. Are your exits, aisles and seating arrangements in order? Are your curtains fireproofed? Are your members, acting and non-acting, covered by insurance against accident? Do you take out a special policy for a non-member brought in in an emergency? Your business manager should make himself acquainted with all the snags. Leave nothing to chance.

The *American National Theatre and Academy* (ANTA), 1545 Broadway, New York 36, N. Y., provides an advisory service for professional actors and amateurs. It is an expert body which can help with every aspect of dramatic work whether of an artistic or administrative nature. Other services received by ANTA members include theatre information, placement and job counseling, photographic loan service, and script service. Members also receive the quarterly *ANTA Newsletter,* 10 issues a year of *World Premieres,* and the *National Theatre Service Pamphlets.* Individual membership is $7.50 per year (tax deductible) and anyone interested in the theatre may join this organization which is nationally chartered by Congress. Whether your organization is a little theatre, a youth club, women's institute, townswomen's guild, a church group or a university, college or school dramatic society, you will find the answer to most of your problems through the *American National Theatre and Academy.*

Glossary

Above-stage. Not applicable in make-shift amateur theatre. In the theatre proper the *flies* and *grid* are above the stage, i.e. behind the top of the *proscenium* and out of sight of the audience.

Act-drop. Usually refers to a painted canvas cloth which is lowered between scenes. It originated in the late eighteenth century to denote the end of an act. The term is now loosely applied to a curtain drawn within the proscenium to separate the stage from the auditorium.

Acting area. Generally the whole of the stage visible to all members of the audience. Or a certain part of the stage used for a particular scene. An 'acting area lantern' is used behind the proscenium to give a vertical beam with a cut-off angle to give extra illumination to a particular acting area.

Ad lib. Extemporary dialogue; words interpolated by an actor in an emergency—a missed entrance, a forgotten cue, an accident on the part of the property master or stage manager.

Alive. A property, piece of scenery or lighting equipment still required during the performance. (*See* **Kill.**)

Apron. The part of the stage or acting area extending into the auditorium in front of the proscenium. Loosely applied to the forestage, between the house-curtain and the footlights.

Backcloth. A hanging canvas used as a background. It can be painted for scenic effect or plain as a sky-cloth where there is no *cyclorama*. In the latter case it can be lighted for various effects.

Backing. A piece of scenery used behind an opening such as a door or a window to conceal stage walls, etc., from the audience.

Backstage. The part of the theatre behind the curtain when it is down. When the curtain is up, during performance, 'backstage' refers to the parts behind the proscenium unseen by the audience; the wings, dressing-rooms, etc.

Barrel. Metal tubing carrying light equipment or scenery, e.g. 'spot-bar', which can be raised or lowered by a system of ropes and pulleys.

Batten. Scenic: a length of timber used on the rope and pulley principle for holding cloths or drapery. Lighting: non-directional lighting compartments illuminating the stage in rows from above and usually masked by *borders*; No. 1 batten is generally the one nearest the front of the stage behind the proscenium.

Black-out. The instant and simultaneous switching off of all stage lights on cue. Not so common in dramatic productions as in revue and musicals.

Block. A pulley, single or double, fixed to a beam or *grid* above stage. (*See* **Barrel** and **Batten**.)

Boat-truck. A low platform on wheels on which scenery can be pre-set off-stage and moved into position on-stage when required.

Board. Switchboard: the electrician operating the lights is said to be 'on the board'.

Boards. The stage floor. Anyone following the profession of acting is sometimes referred to as 'on the boards'. 'I'm treading the boards tonight' means 'I'm performing tonight'.

Book. The stage-manager's copy of the play with all stage directions. 'Who's on "the book" ' means 'who is prompting?'

Book flat. A pair of self-supporting hinged flats, opening and closing like a book.

Border. Canvas or drapery hung at the top of the stage to conceal barrels, battens, lighting equipment or the tops of flats from the audience. Borders can be dual-purpose, plain or painted, straight or shaped to match the rest of the scenery, e.g. foliage border.

Box-set. Flats built to represent three sides of a room or interior setting, with the angle of the side and back wall greater than that of a right-angle to improve *sight-lines*. A complete box-set has a ceiling cloth covering the whole of the acting area though borders are often used instead.

Brace. A strip of timber or metal for supporting flats, one end screwed to the frame of the flat and the other to the floor: for quick-changing, a brace-weight of heavy iron can be used to hold the brace in position on the floor. A brace is also the name of the diagonal piece of wood strengthening the frame and supporting the canvas in the flat itself.

Carpet-cut. A hinged board or trap downstage and parallel with the footlights for securing the front edge of the stage-cloth or carpet.

Chips. Chippy. Nickname used for the stage-carpenter.

Cleat. A metal attachment on the frame of a flat for joining one flat to another by means of a rope or line.

Cue. The last few words spoken by one actor as an indication to the next in turn to speak. A note in the prompt copy for noises off, effects, light changes, etc. A cue-light worked by the stage-manager from the prompt-corner for a member of his team who is out of sight for a hand or other signal.

Cut-cloth. A piece of hanging scenery cut to shape. For the effect of distance a series of canvases with the middles cut out, each hole smaller than the one in front of it and differently shaped, for a woodland scene, eliminates the use of borders and wings.

Cyclorama. A permanent plastered background curved at the sides and top in a dome-like shape for exterior scenes mainly, although the use of projection lanterns can provide scenic effects. The latter are usually beyond the resources of the average amateur groups. A canvas sky-cloth curved at the sides and high enough for the elimination of borders, if well stretched and free from creases, can be almost as effective as the plaster cyclorama.

Dead. Correct, Exact. O.K. When setting scenery, flats, borders, lighting equipment, they are said to be 'dead' when they are in the correct position or properly adjusted.

Dimmer. Apparatus for the gradual increase or decrease of the intensity of light on the whole or part of the stage, or F.O.H.

Dip. A small trap in the stage floor for connecting units of lighting equipment and the concealment and protection of electric plugs. (American: 'pocket'.)

Dock. Scene dock; a space, usually on the stage, for storing scenery.

Double crown. The size of a playbill (30 in. by 20 in.).

Downstage. The front of the stage; nearest the audience.

Drapes. Draperies. Material not framed or stretched. Curtains used as part of the setting.

Drop. A canvas scenic piece dropped from the flies.

False proscenium. Inner proscenium; between the proscenium proper and the beginning of the stage setting—a kind of inner frame. It can be either flats or curtains nowadays and used for downstage entrances.

Fit-up. Touring companies or strolling players with portable equipment suitable for converting any kind of hall into a temporary theatre.

Flat. Covers a wide variety of frames, usually made from 3 in. by 1 in. timber and covered with canvas or material which can be painted. The *Oxford Companion to the Theatre* devotes over two double-column pages to 'Flat'.

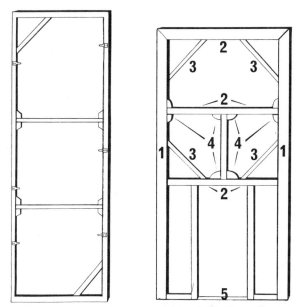

Left: The principle of 'flat' construction; timber frame for canvas. Size dependent on the 'set' or height of stage. Suggested width 5 ft. 9 in. Metal cleats required for tying flats together. A 'flat' used horizontally can be made into a 'ground row' and the canvas on the 'top' edge shaped according to the necessary requirements. *Right:* Diagram showing the back of a 'flat' with a doorframe: wooden frame before canvas surface and door are added. 1, Stile; 2, Rail; 3, Batten; 4, Toggle; 5, Metal plate.

Flies (or **flys**). Galleries above-stage from which scenery is lowered, or lighting apparatus manipulated. Pulleys, counterweights, cleats, lines and general working equipment are controlled on a different level from the one at which the actors are working. Fly-rail or pin-rail; the railing to which the ropes holding the scenery, etc., are secured.

Flipper. The extension to a flat or wing, cut out or shaped and hinged to the flat so that it can be placed at any angle or folded for packing.

Floats. The footlights; usually in a sunken trough running along the front of the stage. So called from the early practice of floating lighted wicks in oil.

Flood. A non-directional or unbeamed lighting unit.

F.O.H. Front-of-house. Normally the auditorium.

Fourth wall. The proscenium opening in the picture frame stage. With a box-set in a realistic drama the audience is supposed to imagine that the fourth wall has been removed for its benefit.

Frost. A piece of gelatine, glass or some such material used in the frame of a lighting unit for dispersal and softening of the beam. A filter for the diffusion of light.

Gauze. Gauze-cloth. Undyed fine net used for special effects. If stretched and weighted to eliminate folds and creases is invisible when lit from behind and opaque when lit from the front. Normally lowered from the flies to cover the whole of the proscenium opening and situated immediately behind the front curtain.

Gelatine. Translucent material used as a colour filter in lighting units such as spots, floods, footlights.

Green-room. Common-room for actors, backstage. Uncommon in amateur theatre and becoming less common in professional.

Grid. Framework above-stage for suspending scenery and equipment.

Ground plan. Working plan of the stage in which positions of scenery, etc. for a particular production are shown.

Ground row. Low pieces of scenery at the back of the stage normally used for exterior scenes, serving the dual purpose of masking ground level lighting for the cyclorama.

Houselights. Auditorium illumination.

House tabs. Tableau curtains; the front or main curtain.

Inner proscenium. *See* **False proscenium** and **Tormentor.**

Inset. A smaller setting for a short scene or a whole act assembled in front of and within the main or larger setting.

Iron. The fire or safety curtain which must by law be lowered once during each performance. Not applicable in amateur theatre.

Jog. American term for the 'return' flat, used to give the impression of thickness to a 'wall', e.g. in a fireplace or recess.

Kill. Remove something no longer required during the performance.

Leg. A piece of canvas or drapery hung and used as a wing.

Legit. Abbreviation for 'legitimate drama' or straight plays, as opposed to revue, musicals, pantomime.

Line. The rope used for 'flying' equipment.

Make-off. Tie-off. Fasten ropes or lines when position is finally decided.

Mask. To obscure from the view of the audience an actor, object or part of the setting which they were intended to see.

Mask-in. Deliberately to obscure from the view of the audience things they are not intended to see.

O.P. Abbreviation for 'opposite prompt side', the side of the stage to the actor's right as he faces the audience.

Pack. A number of flats leaning against the wall of the stage.

Pelmet. The first border, usually more ornamental and better draped than those behind it. The valance at the top of a window frame.

Perch. A small platform just inside the proscenium arch for the operation of lighting units in that position. Perch-spot.

Pilot. A working light, probably a single bulb for use at rehearsal independent of switchboard, or a signal light on the switchboard showing that a circuit is alive.

Projector. Directional lighting unit. Projector lantern or effect projector used with special slides and attachments to provide the effects of cloud, scenery, etc. on the cyclorama.

Prompt corner. Traditionally the corner to the actor's left when facing the audience. The downstage corner immediately behind the proscenium from which the stage manager controls the production; the position taken up by the prompter. Tradition does not always hold for either O.P. or Prompt side in the amateur theatre.

Props. An abbreviation for Property Master, or for properties such as 'hand prop'. The term often covers all articles other than scenery.

Pros. Abbreviation for the proscenium. False pros. The structure which frames the stage and separates it from the auditorium.

Proscenium. The frame and opening between stage and F.O.H.

Rag. Slang for 'curtain'.

Rail. Fly-rail, pin-rail, cleat-rail: in the flies for tying-off. Also the short sides of a flat.

Rake. A rise of about 1 in 24 from the front to the back of the stage floor. Almost obsolete, though the auditorium is generally 'raked'.

Return. A narrow flat used to give the appearance of depth or solidity to a wall when set at right-angles to a wider flat. (*See* **Jog.**)

Reveal. On the principle of the 'return' piece, but smaller and used mainly to sink or give thickness to door and window frames.

Revolve. Revolving stage. Mechanical device on the principle of the turn-table which enables scenes to be pre-set and revolved into position.

Rostrum. A stage platform; higher level than that of stage floor. ('Parallel' in American parlance.)

Set. A noun describing the complete scene; exterior, interior, box, garden, etc. Or a verb meaning to prepare or assemble the pieces—to 'set' the scene. Also the *setting line* beyond which nothing must be placed to foul the curtain.

Sheave. A pulley. (*See* **Block.**)

Sight line. Lines of visibility from the auditorium to the stage.

Sill. The bottom edge of a piece of scenery, usually a flat, especially to the metal or wooden strip at floor level at an entrance or doorway.

Sparks. The popular name for the electrician.

Spot. Lighting unit with directional and variable beam. (*See* **Barrel.**)

Spot Line. A single rope lowered from above-stage to hold articles such as chandeliers.

Spread. Noun: the upward limit of the beam-angle of a spot. Verb: to adjust or widen the beam-angle—'Spread No. 1. F.O.H. spot'.

Stage left. Actor's left side of stage when facing the audience.

Stage right. Actor's right side of stage when facing the audience.

Stage screw. A large screw which can be hand-turned for securing braces.

Stile. The vertical lengths of timber in the frame of a flat.

Strike. To dismantle or remove the setting or single object.

Super. Abbreviation of 'supernumerary'. A non-speaking part.

Swag. To hang with uneven edge; a looped-up curtain or border.

Tail. *See* **Leg.** Or short ends of electric cable on a piece of apparatus ready for connexion to mains supply.

Teaser. The border or horizontal part of the false proscenium.

Throw. The distance between a lighting unit and the object of illumination.

Toggle. Metal or wooden strengtheners attached to the rail and stile of a flat.

Tormentor. Masking flats or curtains immediately inside the proscenium arch. Tormentors and teaser form a false proscenium, which can be adjusted for a smaller setting if the stage is too big for a particular production.

Trap. A cutting in the floor of the stage with hinged flaps or elevator, e.g. grave trap for Hamlet or cauldron trap for Macbeth. Traps are sometimes made in flats and scenery for quick appearances and disappearances.

Trick line. A strong black cord operated manually for special effects during the performance, e.g. falling pictures, doors opening by themselves, objects collapsing, or for quick changes such as opening hinged flats and so forth.

Tripe. Electric cable, especially flexible cable attached to portable lighting apparatus.

Tumbler. A loose rounded batten, or roller, inside a rolled cloth or canvas. The bottom batten which stretches and gives weight to a drop cloth.

Upstage. The part of the stage farthest away from the audience. Also, to 'upstage' another actor is to force him to turn his back on the audience to deliver a line.

Walk-on. *See* **Super.**

Wing. A flat at the side of the stage for masking off-stage.

Bibliography

Actors on Acting, Cole and Chinoy.
An Actor Prepares, Constantin Stanislavski.
Building a Character, Constantin Stanislavski.
Reflections on the Theatre, Jean Louis Barrault.
Prefaces to Shakespeare, Harley Granville-Barker.
What Happens in Hamlet, John Dover Wilson.
The Essential Shakespeare, John Dover Wilson.
Editions of Shakespeare's plays, John Dover Wilson.
Theatre in Soviet Russia, André van Gyseghem.
Historic Costume for the Stage, Lucy Barton.
English Costume, Iris Brook (7 volumes).
A Dictionary of English Costume (900–1900), Cunnington and Beard.
The Amateur Actor, Frances Mackenzie.
A Year's Course in Speech Training, Anne McAllister.
Stage Properties, Heather Conway.
Playing Period Plays, Lyn Oxenford.
The Oxford Companion to the Theatre, Phyllis Hartnoll.
Stage Scenery and Lighting, Selden and Sellman.
Stage Lighting, Ridge and Aldred.
Stage Planning and Equipment, P. Corry.
Designing for the Stage, Doris Zinkeisen.

Index

157